Quod scriptura, non iubet vetat

The Latin translates, "What is not commanded in scripture, is forbidden:'

On the Cover: Baptists rejoice to hold in common with other evangelicals the main principles of the orthodox Christian faith. However, there are points of difference and these differences are significant. In fact, because these differences arise out of God's revealed will, they are of vital importance. Hence, the barriers of separation between Baptists and others can hardly be considered a trifling matter. To suppose that Baptists are kept apart solely by their views on Baptism or the Lord's Supper is a regrettable misunderstanding. Baptists hold views which distinguish them from Catholics, Congregationalists, Episcopalians, Lutherans, Methodists, Pentecostals, and Presbyterians, and the differences are so great as not only to justify, but to demand, the separate denominational existence of Baptists. Some people think Baptists ought not teach and emphasize their differences but as E.J. Forrester stated in 1893, "Any denomination that has views which justify its separate existence, is bound to promulgate those views. If those views are of sufficient importance to justify a separate existence, they are important enough to create a duty for their promulgation ... the very same reasons which justify the separate existence of any denomination make it the duty of that denomination to teach the distinctive doctrines upon which its separate existence rests." If Baptists have a right to a separate denominational life, it is their duty to propagate their distinctive principles, without which their separate life cannot be justified or maintained.

Many among today's professing Baptists have an agenda to revise the Baptist distinctives and redefine what it means to be a Baptist. Others don't understand why it even matters. The books being reproduced in the *Baptist Distinctives Series* are republished in order that Baptists from the past may state, explain and defend the primary Baptist distinctives as they understood them. It is hoped that this Series will provide a more thorough historical perspective on what it means to be distinctively Baptist.

The Lord Jesus Christ asked, *"And why call ye me, Lord, Lord, and do not the things which I say?"* (Luke 6:46). The immediate context surrounding this question explains what it means to be a true disciple of Christ. Addressing the same issue, Christ's question is meant to show that a confession of discipleship to the Lord Jesus Christ is inconsistent and untrue if it is not accompanied with a corresponding submission to His authoritative commands. Christ's question teaches us that a true recognition of His authority as Lord inevitably includes a submission to the authority of His Word. Hence, with this question Christ has made it forever impossible to separate His authority as King from the authority of His Word. These two principles—the authority of Christ as King and the authority of His Word—are the two most fundamental Baptist distinctives. The first gives rise to the second and out of these two all the other Baptist distinctives emanate. As F.M. Iams wrote in 1894, "Loyalty to Christ as King, manifesting itself in a constant and unswerving obedience to His will as revealed in His written Word, is the real source of all the Baptist distinctives:' In the search for the *primary* Baptist distinctive many have settled on the Lordship of Christ as the most basic distinctive. Strangely, in doing this, some have attempted to separate Christ's Lordship from the authority of Scripture, as if you could embrace Christ's authority without submitting to what He commanded. However, while Christ's Lordship and Kingly authority can be isolated and considered essentially for discussion's sake, we see from Christ's own words in Luke 6:46 that His Lordship is really inseparable from His Word and, with regard to real Christian discipleship, there can be no practical submission to the one without a practical submission to the other.

In the symbol above the Kingly Crown and the Open Bible represent the inseparable truths of Christ's Kingly and Biblical authority. The Crown and Bible graphics are supplemented by three Bible verses (Ecclesiastes 8:4, Matthew 28:18-20, and Luke 6:46) that reiterate and reinforce the inextricable connection between the authority of Christ as King and the authority of His Word. The truths symbolized by these components are further emphasized by the Latin quotation - *quod scriptura, non iubet vetat*— i.e., "What is not commanded in scripture, is forbidden:' This Latin quote has been considered historically as a summary statement of the regulative principle of Scripture. Together these various symbolic components converge to exhibit the two most foundational Baptist Distinctives out of which all the other Baptist Distinctives arise. Consequently, we have chosen this composite symbol as a logo to represent the primary truths set forth in the *Baptist Distinctives Series*.

The Distinguishing Doctrines of Baptists

J. B. MOODY
1838-1931

The Distinguishing Doctrines of Baptists

By J.B. MOODY, D.D.,

With a Biographical Sketch of the Author by John Franklin Jones

A SERIES OF LECTURES DELIVERED AT THE SOUTHWESTERN BAPTIST UNIVERSITY, JACKSON, TENN., AND AFTERWARDS PUBLISHED IN THE BAPTIST AND REFLECTOR, NASHVILLE, TENN.

NASHVILLE, TENN.
FOLK AND BROWDER PRINT.
1901

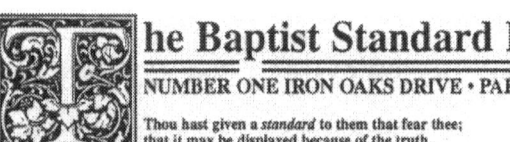

The Baptist Standard Bearer, Inc.
NUMBER ONE IRON OAKS DRIVE • PARIS, ARKANSAS 72855

Thou hast given a *standard* to them that fear thee;
that it may be displayed because of the truth.
-- Psalm 60:4

Reprinted 2006

by

THE BAPTIST STANDARD BEARER, INC.
No. 1 Iron Oaks Drive
Paris, Arkansas 72855
(479) 963-3831

THE WALDENSIAN EMBLEM
lux lucet in tenebris
"The Light Shineth in the Darkness"

ISBN# 1579785255

TABLE OF CONTENTS[1]

CHAPTER
1. INTRODUCTION 1

   DIVISION 1. FOUNDATIONAL PRINCIPLES:
   THE SPIRITUALITY OF RELIGION

   PART 1. DISCERNING BETWEEN THE LETTER
   AND THE SPIRIT IN SCRIPTURE

2. BOTH LAW AND GOSPEL CONSIST OF BOTH NATURAL
   AND SPIRITUAL 7
3. DISCERNING LETTER AND SPIRIT AND BIBLICAL
   ILLUSTRATIONS 12
4. DISCERNING LETTER AND SPIRIT: ADDITIONAL BIBLICAL
   ILLUSTRATIONS 19
5. DISCERNING LETTER AND SPIRIT: FURTHER BIBLICAL
   ILLUSTRATIONS 24
6. DISCERNING LETTER AND SPIRIT IN TYPOLOGY 30
7. FURTHER BIBLICAL ILLUSTRATIONS OF THE PRINCIPLE . 35

   PART 2. DISCERNING BETWEEN THE NATURAL
   AND THE SPIRITUAL IN MAN

8. THE DUAL NATURE OF THE REGENERATE MAN 44
9. DISTINGUISHING NATURAL MORALITY FROM
   REGENERATE SPIRITUALITY 52
10. DISCERNING THE NATURAL FROM THE SPIRITUAL IN THE
    SPIRITUAL MAN: MOTIVES AND EMOTIONS 61

PART 3. DISCERNING BETWEEN THE FORMAL AND THE SPIRITUAL IN RELIGION

11. THE FORMAL AND THE SPIRITUAL IN THE INTERNALS OF RELIGION 69

12. THE FORMAL AND THE SPIRITUAL IN THE EXTERNALS OF RELIGION 75

DIVISION 2. DOCTRINAL / PRACTICAL: REGENERATE CHURCH MEMBERSHIP

13. REGENERATION/CONVERSION ESSENTIAL TO CHURCH MEMBERSHIP 85

14. REGENERATED CHURCH MEMBERSHIP: FURTHER BIBLICAL EVIDENCE 92

15. CHURCH CONSTITUTION: THE NATURE OF THE CHURCH AS CONGREGATIONAL/LOCAL, NOT UNIVERSAL 102

16. THE NATURE OF THE CHURCH AS CONGREGATION/ LOCAL: FURTHER BIBLICAL EVIDENCE 110

17. THE NATURE OF THE CHURCH AS CONGREGATION/ LOCAL: EXAMINATION OF BIBLICAL TEXTS USED TO ADVOCATE THE CHURCH AS UNIVERSAL 120

18. CHURCH GOVERNMENT: THE DIVINE MARKS OF BIBLICAL CONGREGATIONS AND THE CONGREGATION FEATURE 131

19. CHURCH AUTONOMY IN RECEIVING/EXCLUDING MEMBERS 140

20. CHURCH AUTONOMY IN ELECTING OFFICERS 149

21. CHURCH AUTONOMY IN ELECTING ELDERS, PRESBYTERS, OR BISHOPS 157

22. THE FAILURE TO EXTEND AUTHORITY TO THE ENTIRE CONGREGATION 165

23. PARITY AMONG MINISTERS: THE ERROR OF DISTINGUISHING "RULING" AND "TEACHING" ELDERS . . 173

24. PARITY AMONG MINISTERS: THE NEGATIVE MEANING
    OF "RULE OVER" (HEBREWS 13:7, 17, 24) 183

25. PARITY AMONG MINISTERS: THE POSITIVE MEANING OF
    "RULE OVER" (HEBREWS 13:7, 17, 24) 191

26. CHURCHES AS CUSTODIANS OF GOSPEL
    DOCTRINES/ORDINANCES 198

---

[1]The original text had no Table of Contents and few chapter headings. Accordingly, for the benefit of the reader, the Publisher attaches this Table of Contents, prepared by John Franklin Jones, Cordova, TN, August 2006.

"THE LETTER AND THE SPIRIT."

INTRODUCTION.

CHAPTER I.

The circumstances in which I find myself this evening are well calculated to excite the moods of any man as Moody as I am. Appearing as a teacher in a great University, having a Savage president, with a H'Eagle at his right, and a Crook to his back; in Jackson, a name synonymous with "Old Hickory;" in Tennessee, a name having not eyes, yet "see;" with other professors of great wisdom and experience; having many teachers for my pupils—why it is enough to throw a Moody man's moods into the jim jams. I hesitate to assume the positiveness of the Indicative; I dare not venture on the authority of the Imperative: or the liberties of the Infinitive; but must subside into the doubts and uncertainties of the Subjunctive; for I find myself subjoined to a great faculty, with a tremendous emphasis on the Sub.

Three mistakes have been made: First, in inviting me to this work; second, in my accepting; and third, in my coming. I feel like spending half my time in making apologies, and for the rest, beg to be excused. I am embarrassed by the announcements that have been made, and the expectations that have been aroused. You have "Doctrinal Lectures" associated in your minds with Dr. J. R. Graves, whose head and heart were taxed for almost a lifetime in preparing and in perfecting such lectures, and who spent much of his time in delivering them before admiring multitudes, with the added power of inimitable eloquence. Recently I heard two of our greatest orators—Debs and Bryan. It was evident that the speeches were the result of growth—perfected by a thousand deliverances. And so of Dr. Graves and others who have lifted the standard so high, and with it your expectations. Remember, I am not before you with grown lectures, polished and perfected by long practice. Nor have I the inspiring multitudes, with the liberties of oratory if I had it. I am in a school-room to teach, and teaching is done by talking, not by oratory. The acorn has yet to be planted, and if there is an oak in it, it has yet to grow. So please disassociate entirely from your minds the expectations belonging to the aforesaid occasions. I desire as best I can offer you a few suggestions on the study of the Bible, which I trust may lead to the right understanding of Bible Doctrines. From right causes, right effects may be expected.

In all great buildings, care should be taken in laying the foundation; and in all great undertakings there is preparatory work. Christ spoke of digging deep and laying the foundation on a rock; and Paul spoke of laying the foundation, and another building thereon. So I must look after the foundation and the preparatory work, and others will give heed to how and what they build thereon.

I propose to begin with the foundation principles of sound doctrine. Some may expect me to expound and explain Landmarkism, but this I would not dare do without first showing upon what the doctrine rests. No one can take Lankmarkism and Close Communion out of their settings, and commend them acceptably to anybody. Set up these doctrines on sand and any opposition will overthrow them. It is unwise to shake them as rattling skeletons before a liberalized generation. Dogmatic Liberalism can whip out dogmatic Landmarkism with one hand, and not half try. Landmarks are not set by ignorance, but by true bearings and correct measurements, and are maintained by authority. Liberalism scorns boundaries, and laughs at authorities, and condemns records as old and musty and out of fashion. Let us lay the foundation of sound doctrine, then Landmarkism and Close Communion will take care of themselves. In their places, and properly adjusted to other doctrines, they "are things of beauty and a joy forever."

There is a system of doctrine, and I care not to defend any doctrine that does not rightly belong to that system. Indeed, I reject all doctrines that are inconsistent with other doctrines, and that do not harmonize with a system of doctrine taught in the Word. When Paul laid down a startling premise he asked: "What then," or "what shall we say then," and he boldly pressed his way to the logical and theological conclusion. Conclusions are never to be assumed or begged. They result from force, coercive force. The man who cleaves to a premise and abhors the conclusion, is ignorant or dishonest. Let your doctrines be consistent, and your speech and practice consistent with your doctrines. Honesty and faithfulness require this. You had better be nobody—you had better be nothing, than to be inconsistent. I want that to stick.

In your investigations and preaching emphasize the most important doctrines, but never so as to neutralize even the least important. Christ says: "Teach them to guard safely all things whatsoever I have commanded you." And again: "Ye are my friends if ye do whatsoever I command you." There are commandments which may be called the greatest, and others the least; but all have their absolute and relative importance. The feeblest member in the body is important, and must not be destroyed because not as useful as others. From such like folly has come the erroneous idea of nonessential in doctrine. No member of the body is nonessential. While the ear is not essential to the discrimination of colors, nor the eye to that of sounds, yet the eye can't say to the ear, I have no need of you. And so of systematic doctrine.

But doctrines have their relative as well as absolute importance. When seeing is needed the eye is the most important; when hearing, the ear; when walking, the feet; when working, the hands; when talking, the tongue; when breathing, the lungs; and so of all the rest. Each is important and essential in its place. And with tremendous emphasis let me say that so it is, and much more so, with the doctrines of Christ. "The body of divinity" is worth more than millions of human bodies. Now let me burn indelibly in your minds and memories, this scripture: "He that is unfaithful in that which is least, is unfaithful also in much." You must watch the little foxes that gnaw the vines. Some diseases are more fatal than others, yet the least dangerous deserves the most attention when it becomes epidemic. So in the providence of God the less important doctrines are often thrust to the front, and that calls for our greater consideration. The doctor that disdains his patient because he has not the leprosy is as foolish as the preacher who apologizes for dancing because it is not as bad as murder. Atheism, Unitarianism, Universalism, Mormonism, and other isms are damnable heresies; but if these are not in your bounds, and there is an epidemic of the lesser hurtful isms, then duty calls you to the lesser. I would rather give attention to the flea that is annoying my back, than to the fox that is not eating my grapes. The black snake in the house is more dangerous than the rattle snake in the jungles. The errors that Christ and the apostles opposed most were those that were doing the most harm. But these remarks are intended to apply to the practical use of doctrines. Doctrines have their absolute importance, and it is to these I would first claim your attention.

There are doctrines that are vital; that are essential to life. If all doctrines were essential to life, then who could be saved? If no doctrine was essential to life, then who could be lost? When Christ said, "Ye have no life in you," he was not referring to the life of the natural man, but to spiritual life, the life we lost in Adam. Christ came to restore spiritual life and light more abundantly. "Except a man be born again he cannot see the kingdom of God." "That which is born of the flesh is flesh and that which is born of the Spirit is spirit." The birth of the flesh produces the natural man with his mental and moral perceptions. A great editor recently stated that the natural man was morally dead. This a great mistake. He is only spiritually dead. The birth of the Spirit gives spiritual life and spiritual perceptions. (1 Cor. ii. 14). Vital doctrines are spiritual doctrines, and are of the greatest absolute importance. With these let us begin our search, and let us seek not only spiritual knowledge but spiritual enjoyment.

We will begin with contrasts and comparisons, which greatly facilitate our learning. If time permitted I would like to exercise our senses in discerning moral good and evil; but for want of time, we will have to begin with spiritual things. First, let us discern between the Letter and Spirit of the Bible. Second, let us discern between that which is Natural and that which is Spiritual in man. Third, let us try to discern between the Formal and the Spiritual in religion.

This will afford a field of spiritual survey in which, by the right exercise of our discerning senses, we will become more skillful in the word of righteousness. Here is neglected ground which needs to be cleared up before we can well till it. Here is the beginning of "Distinctive Baptist Doctrines." It includes Regenerated Church Membership, which is the prime plank in our doctrinal and practical platform. There should be no church membership without regeneration, and no regenerated person should be without church membership; and church membership should be in an institution just like the one Christ built, organized on the same principles and for the same purposes. Let us spend a few days on the spirituality of religion involved in the term regeneration; and the rest of the time we will spend on the doctrinal and practical features of religion as taught in the Word and believed by Baptists, and which are contained in the words—"Church Membership." This will lead to the discussion of the church question, with its Constitution, Polity, Ordinances, Doctrines, Duties, etc. But let us first become thoroughly imbued with the spirituality of religion before coming to its forms and doctrines, and these must be made spiritual, or they will prove a bane and not a blessing.

CHAPTER II.

The doctrine of Regenerated Church Membership is both important and comprehensive. If Christ limited church membership to regenerated persons it was because regeneration was necessary to the purpose of church membership. The church was instituted for worship and for service, and both worship and service were to be spiritual; hence the spiritual qualification of regeneration was necessary. The natural man is not spiritual, nor is the religion of the natural man spiritual, nor can it be. As the Bible, including both law and gospel, is for the whole world, including both saints and sinners, it must be adapted to both. So there is that in the Bible adapted to the natural man, and which the natural man can understand; and there is that adapted to the spiritual man, and which he alone can understand. Hence we read of the letter and the spirit of the law—old covenant (Rom. vii. 6); and also the letter and the spirit of the new covenant (2 Cor. iii. 6). The letter, if it leads the natural man at all, leads him into formal worship and service. As the natural man can't discern spiritual things (1 Cor. ii. 14), he can't discern the spirituality of the law nor of the gospel, nor the spirituality of worship and service; and as God is Spirit and must be worshiped in spirit and in truth, man must become spiritual; that is, born of the Spirit, and birth of the Spirit is regeneration. Not till then can man see the spiritual kingdom of God and the spiritual things of the kingdom (Rom. xiv. 17, 18). The Bible, containing both letter and spirit, is an all-sufficient guide to the spiritual man in both the forms and spirit of religion. Then let us study the two fold nature of this wonderful book.

The Scripture to be especially studied at this point is 2 Cor. ii 14 to iv. 7. As King James' Version is faulty and misleading on some important points, I recommend the Improved Edition of the American

Bible Union Version by Broadus, Weston and Hovey. Chapter iii. 5, 6 reads: "Not that we are sufficient of ourselves to think anything as from ourselves; but our sufficiency is of God; who also made us sufficient as ministers of a new covenant; not of the letter, but of the Spirit; for the letter kills, but the Spirit makes alive." Rom. vii. 6 reads: "But now we have been loosed from the law, having died to that in which we were held; so that we serve in newness of spirit and not in oldness of letter." I have taken the liberty to drop the article before spirit and letter according to the Greek. Newness and oldness characterize the kinds of service rendered before and after the "deliverance," in which we died to the slavery of mere formal service to the letter, and became alive to voluntary, delightful and spiritual service. Note, the change is not from the formal service of the law to the spiritual service of the gospel, or the formal service of the old covenant to the spiritual service of the new covenant; but the reference is to two kinds of service to the law. In our natural state, while dead in trespasses and in sins, being under law as a principle of life and justification, all of our obedience was counted dead works. But when we died to sin, and became alive unto God (by regeneration), then we serve the law not in oldness of letter, but in newness of spirit. That is, we "consent unto the law that it is good," and we "delight in the law of God after the inward man (which was begotten or created by regeneration). The law having given us a knowledge of sin—of our own sin and condemnation, and having "tutored" us through its prophecies, types, and sacrifices, unto Christ, as the mediator of a better covenant—then we were no longer under law as a principle of justification, yet we continue to serve the law, not in oldness of letter but in newness of spirit. Without this change of spirit in service, the natural man could join the church, be baptized, and go through all the role and round of religious duties under the new covenant according to the letter.

But this formal, heartless, faithless service to both law and gospel would be dead works and would end in death. The righteousness of our obedience to the letter of both law and gospel might be blameless, yet without this newness of spirit in obedience, which came of "being made alive unto God," the end would be death. "The letter kills." The letter of both covenants kills. Hence to bring an unregenerated man into the church for the perfunctory performance of letter service is bringing him to a double death; to a condemnation of both law and gospel; for both being spiritual, require a spiritual service. If Christ's church is to be a spiritual temple, "to offer spiritual service, holy and acceptable unto God," then woe to the uncircumcised in heart who defile the temple of God; and woe to those who knowingly bring them in. If the temple of God is to be holy, built up of spiritual stones, to bring in other material is to destroy the temple of God; and "if any man destroys the temple of God, him will God destroy." (1 Cor.

iii. 16, 17). If the temple is not spiritual, it is not God's temple.

The stones in Solomon's temple were prepared for the temple, but before being brought to the temple. So the spiritual stones for the spiritual temple must be prepared (by regeneration) for the temple, but before being brought to the temple. If God ordains "living stones to be built into a spiritual temple," then woe to him who puts unliving (dead) stones into it. And as the stones were prepared for the temple, and of no service apart from the temple, so these spiritual stones were prepared (by new creation) for the temple, and apart from the temple they can not subserve the purpose of their new creation. Hence all the regenerated must go into the house of the Lord, and no other kind. "The Lord added to the church daily the saved."

Whenever and wherever a man believes in Jesus to the saving of his soul, let him walk if necessary 60 miles to receive a "baptism from heaven" and not "of men" and at the hands of one sent of God to baptize, and thus follow his Lord's example. And wherever two or three baptized disciples abide, there they ought to "gather together in Christ's name," and organize, and co-operate. They should take Christ as their only head, and lawgiver, and teacher, and they should bind themselves to be governed in all things by his word and to his way; interpreting that word for themselves but not by themselves, but seek ever to understand the will of the Lord by the Holy Spirit promised to them. Then they will be guided into a knowledge of spiritual truth. Yea the Spirit will take of the things of Jesus, contained in the letter of the law and gospel, and will reveal it unto them. My earnest desire and prayer to God is, that those who read these lines may be filled with the "exact knowledge" of his will, in all spiritual wisdom and understanding; that they may walk worthy of the Lord, in all things pleasing him; being strenghtened with all power, according to the might of his glory, unto all patience and longsuffering with joy, giving thanks to the Father who made us meet for the portion of the inheritance of the saints in light. (Col. i. 9-12). But spiritual wisdom and understanding must be sought.

NOTE.—I write these articles from the notes from which I spoke. But what I spoke I know not, and what I will write I know not. I will go over the same ground, in about the same way, leaving my mind as free to write as it was to speak. This is all the likeness I can promise.

CHAPTER III.

Many things that are much alike are more unlike, and education teaches us to discern the difference. A druggist should know the difference in medicines, especially those that have some resemblance. Sand and sugar may look alike, but they don't taste alike. For eating purposes there is a difference, and the difference is important to discern. The moral world is chaos to those who have no moral discernment. Yet " woe be to them that call evil good and good evil." (Isa. v. 20). If a man fail to discern between good and evil, between food and poison, he must take the consequences. God gives time and talents that we may learn to discern between things that differ, and if we learn not, our ignorance is both culpable and damnable. If there is such difference between the Letter and Spirit, that one kills and the other makes alive, then those who fail to discern the difference must receive the awful penalty of the "second death, which is the lake of fire and brimstone," "to be tormented forever and ever." (Rev. xx. 10, 15).

God made the animals to breathe the air. Man is an animal and also breathes the air. But he is more than an animal, and breathes more than air. He breathes the breath of God (Gen. ii. 7). When animals cease to breathe the air, they live no more; but when man ceases to breathe the air, he lives on, for he is a living soul. So the Bible is to be distinguished from all other books, because God breathed into it the breath of life (2 Tim. iii. 16); so that it "lives and abides forever" (1 Pet. i. 23). "It is living, and powerful, sharper than any two-edged sword, piercing even to the dividing asunder of soul and spirit, and the joints and the marrow, and is a discerner of the thoughts and intents of the heart" (Heb. iv. 12). As there is something in man that makes him greater and more abiding than animals, so there is something in the Bible that makes it greater and more abiding than other books. Like other books, it has form and letter and natural meaning, but it has more. It has Spirit, for God breathed into its nostrils and it became a living Book. It is to be interpreted like other books as far as it goes, and the man that can't see any more is a natural man, and can't discern the spiritual things prepared for us and revealed to us by His Spirit, who inspired the Word, and then begat in us spiritual life and discernment.

The professing Christian world is to-day full of letter knowledge and "forms of godliness," but there is a dearth and destitution of spirit and power. A vail is on the Scriptures, both old and new, and zealous formalists have their minds blinded. To them the gospel, which is the power of God unto salvation, is hid, and the light of the glorious gospel of Christ does not shine into their hearts to give them the light of the knowledge of the glory of God in the face of Jesus Christ (2 Cor. iv. 4-6). They are clothed in the armor of self-righteousness on the right hand and on the left, and they are like the Pharisees, sounding a trumpet when giving alms, to be seen of men; praying in synagogues and on the corners of the streets; fasting with sad countenances and disfigured faces and dissheveled hair; tithing mint, anise and cummin; binding heavy burdens and grievous to be borne and laying them on other men's shoulders; making broad their phylacteries and enlarging the borders of their garments; loving the uppermost seats, and greetings, and high sounding titles; and for a pretense they read long and many prayers, for which they will receive the greater damnation; compassing land and sea to make one proselyte; esteeming gold greater than the temple and the gift greater than the altar; making clean the outside of the cup and platter; honoring the prophets and martyrs and condemning their murder, yet allying themselves to the "Mother Church," which is the "Mother of Harlots," thus partaking with them in the blood of the witnesses of Jesus; full of outward righteousness that appear beautiful unto men, while they continue to fill up the measure of the apostate church, which has corrupted the right ways of the Lord in all the earth. These false teachers have privily brought in damnable heresies, speaking evil of the way of truth, and through coveteousness, with feigned words, they make merchandise of men, whose judgment now of a long time lingereth not and their damnation slumbereth not. (2 Pet. ii. 4). Prophecy foretold and history corroborates the source and sum and substance of this formalism that has denied the faith as well as the power of godliness. From all such let us turn away.

These ritualists have forms of piety and godliness. They have houses of worship, built to be seen of men; singing and preaching and praying to be heard of men; ordinances to be received of men; doctrines to please men; zeal to catch men, and treasuries to be filled by men. What natural men demand they have abundantly supplied. Not having the spirit they magnify the letter, and multiply the forms. Spiritual discernment is the only remedy.

Spiritual truth must be discerned. It is contained in the Word of God, and may He open our understandings that we may understand the Scriptures.

Notice first, the expression, "Not of the Letter but of the Spirit." This does not mean not at all of the letter, but rather not alone of the letter. It is an emphatic contrast, placing the superlative importance on the Spirit, so that the letter without the Spirit is nothing. This is strikingly confirmed in the 9th and 10th verses: "For if the ministration of condemnation has glory, much more does the ministration of righteousness exceed in glory. For that which has been made glorious has not been made glorious in this respect, on account of the glory that excels. (2 Cor. iii. 9-10). A tallow candle gives light, but when compared to a search light, it has no light, by reason of the light that excels. When David said (Ps. li.4): "Against thee, thee only have I sinned," the meaning is, that his sin against God was of such superlative magnitude that his sin against Uriah was nothing. So Peter in Acts. v. 4, said: "Ye have not lied unto men but unto God." Ananias had lied unto men, but that was nothing when compared to his lie unto God. We should not fear men, for they can only kill the body, but we should fear Him who after he hath killed, has power to destroy both soul and body in hell. When Christ said labor not for the food that perishes, he did not mean that they should not labor at all, but they should not labor alone for that. The emphasis is on the food that endures with everlasting life;

and so great is that emphasis that the expression is justifiable—"Labor not for the food that perishes, but for that that endures unto everlasting life." (John vi. 27). We walk by faith and not by sight, is to be interpreted the same way. The same with "Love not in word and tongue, but in deed and in truth." It does not mean love not at all in word and tongue, but not alone, putting the superlative importance on loving in deed and in truth. Loving alone in word and tongue killeth, but loving also in deed and in truth gives life.

So Paul was made a minister not of the Letter alone, but also of the Spirit, with the superlative importance on the Spirit. For the letter alone killeth, but the Spirit with the letter makes alive. The letter and the Spirit are related like the body and the Spirit, the acorn and the oak, the hull and the kernel, the corn and the shuck. We should minister to the body for the soul's sake, to the hull for the kernel's sake, to the shuck for the corn's sake, and to the acorn for the oak's sake. And here I will anticipate enough to say that I would not defend the action of baptism for the form's sake, but for the sake of that implied in the form. Of itself, one physical action is no better than another. I believe the last baptism "in the Spirit" is recorded in the 19th chapter of Acts, yet I believe in spiritual baptism. That is, I believe there is both letter and Spirit in baptism, and that the letter without the Spirit is nothing; and worse, for it has killed its multiplied millions. And so with every other religious service, as I will try to show when we come to discern between the Formal and Spiritual in religion.

And so I believe in observing the letter of the Scriptures, but not the letter only, but also, and especially, and emphatically, and superlatively, the Spirit. Let us next try to develop this distinction, and see what a wonderful life-giving book is the Book of God.

Perhaps the greatest difficulty to overcome is the prejudice excited by the extravagant spiritualizing of Swedenborg, who spiritualized in disregard of the letter. While I loath the foolish spiritualizing of Swedenborg, yet I will not let this drive me from that spiritualizing which is in harmony with the letter.

"Now the Lord is that Spirit." "And we all with unvailed face beholding as in a mirror the glory of the Lord are changed into the same image from glory to glory, as by the Spirit the Lord." (2 Cor. iii. 17-18.)

Now turn and read John i. 1-10 ; Eph. iii. 9; Col. i. 16; Heb. 1:10; Rev. iv. 11, and then turn to the first chapter of Genesis and discern "the Spirit, the Lord" in the "us" and the "our" of verse 26, and also in God —Elohim (plural) of the first verse. When you read the first chapter of Genesis, say: "I would see Jesus," and pray the Father and the Spirit, always recognized in the first two verses, saying, "Show us the Son and it sufficeth us."

Chapter IV.

Having found "the Lord, the Spirit" of the letter in the first chapter of Genesis, let us search diligently for him in the second chapter, especially from the 18th to 24th verses : " And the Lord God said, It is not good that the man should be alone; I will make him a help meet for him. And out of the ground the Lord God formed every beast of the field, and every fowl of the air; and brought them unto Adam to see what he would call them: and whatsoever Adam called every living creature, that was the name thereof. And Adam gave names to all cattle, and to the fowl of the air, and to every beast of the field; but for Adam there was not found a help meet for him. And the Lord God caused a deep sleep to fall upon Adam, and he slept; and he took one of his ribs, and closed up the flesh instead thereof. And the rib, which the Lord God had taken from man, made he a woman, and brought her unto the man. And Adam said, This is now bone of my bones, and flesh of my flesh: she shall be called Woman, because she was taken out of man. Therefore shall a man leave his father and his mother, and shall cleave unto his wife: and they shall be one flesh."

The letter is plain. It is a truthful, historical account of the creation of Adam and Eve. I believe the literal, historical narrative. I believe all of that, but I believe there is more in it than that. I believe according to Rev. xix. 10, that "the testimony of Jesus is the spirit of prophecy;" and that the testimony of Jesus is the spirit of history; and that the testimony of Jesus is the spirit of nature (Ps. xix. 1-6); and that the testimony of Jesus is the spirit of the law; and that the testimony of Jesus is the spirit of ordinances; and that the testimony of Jesus is the spirit of types and symbols and shadows; of the rock, manna, Rock, brazen serpent, sacrifices, temple, baptism, the supper; yea, the testimony of Jesus should be the spirit of every redeemed life. We should see Jesus in the High Priest, in David, in Solomon, in Moses, and in Paul, who said: "I no longer live, but Christ lives in me." (Gal. ii. 20). If we put on Christ, and are clothed with Christ, then should not the spirit of every saint's life be, " the testimony of Jesus?"

Now let us go back to the Scripture quoted, and search for the spirit of the letter, in comparison with which the historical fact is nothing. If the Letter were all, there would be nothing in it to give spiritual life and hope to us. (Rom. xv. 4). Happily we have an inspired commentary on this Scripture. Paul by the Holy Spirit saw in Adam a second Adam, and in Eve a spiritual woman for the spiritual man. That spiritual man was Christ Jesus, and that spiritual woman was the church; and the relation that subsisted between Adam and Eve, yea between every husband and wife, is to testify of the relation between Christ and his church. Let us read Eph. v. 21-33 : "Submitting yourselves to one another in the fear of Christ; wives to their own husbands, as to the Lord. Because a husband is head of the wife, as also Christ is head of the church; himself the Savior of the body. But as the church is subject to Christ, so also are the wives to their own husbands in everything. Husbands, love your wives, as also Christ loved the church, and delivered himself up for it; that he might sanctify it, having cleansed it by the bathing of water in the word, that he might himself present to himself the church, glorious, not having a spot, or wrinkle, or any such thing, but that it may be holy and without blemish. So husbands ought to love their own wives as their own bodies. He that loves his own wife loves himself. For no one ever hated his own flesh; but nourishes and cherishes it, even as Christ the church; because we are members of his body. For this cause shall a man leave father and mother, and shall cleave to his wife, and the two shall be one flesh. This mystery is great; but I am speaking of Christ and of the church. Nevertheless do ye also, severally, each so love his own wife even as himself; and let the wife see that she reverence her husband."

Note, the 31st verse is a quotation of Gen. ii. 24: "For this cause shall a man leave father and mother, and shall cleave unto his wife, and they two shall be one flesh." Then he says, "This is a great mystery, but I speak concerning Christ and the church;" and the next verse teaches us that while Paul spiritualized the passage quoted, yet he did not spiritualize the letter away, for he says: " Nevertheless do ye also, severally, each so love his own wife even as himself; and let the wife see that she reverence her husband."

Every husband and wife should realize that they are living types of Christ and his church. When they live thus, and always act thus, then their married relation and lives are spiritual, and they glorify Christ in the holy ordinance which was appointed for that purpose. When we nourish and cherish our wives, we should do so to show that Christ nourishes and cherishes his church. When wives submit in all social matters to their husbands, their motive ought to be to show that in all things the church should be subject to Christ. And as Christ laid down his life for the church, so husbands ought to lay down their lives, if need be, for their wives. If wives should learn with all subjection to submit to their husbands, and to wear long hair for a veil or covering, and not to exercise authority over their husbands, it should be for these reasons; first, Adam was first formed, then Eve; second, the man was not formed for the woman, but the woman for the man; third, the woman was first in transgression; and fourth, the wife is the weaker vessel. These are the natural reasons, binding on all natural wives. But if a wife is spiritual, she should especially do these things in order to show the subjection of the church to Christ in all things.

I must humbly beg leave to suggest that our translators erred in 1 Tim. ii. 11, 12, and in 1 Cor. xi. 3 by translating man and woman instead of husband and wife. In Eph. v. 23 they say rightly that the husband is the head of the wife, but in 1 Cor. xi. 3 they say that the man is the head of the woman. The Greek being the same, we are left to the context to decide when to translate man or husband, and woman or wife, there being no Greek for husband and wife. Now if the man, as a man, is the head of the woman, as a woman, then any man is the head of any woman; yea, every man is the head of any woman; and the wife being a woman, every man is the head of every wife, and so the husband in no particular sense can be the head of his wife. I don't believe that any man is the head of any woman. I don't believe that any unmarried man is the head of every unmarried and married woman. I don't believe the Holy Spirit taught any such impractical foolishness. If man and woman are to be retained as the proper translations in these places, it must be on the ground that they were formed for the married relation; and "to bear children" (1 Tim. ii. 15) not as women, but as wives. This is made clear enough in 1 Cor. xiv. 34, 35: "Let your women keep silence in the churches . . . And if they will learn anything let them ask their husbands at home." So the women referred to in verse 34 had husbands, and the law that made the wife subject unto her husband must be maintained under the gospel, and especially in the church. The law and the gospel allow wives to exercise their spiritual gifts—and even in the church they could pray and prophecy with their heads covered, as a sign of subjection to their husbands, but when a dispute is up about the greater gifts or anything involving authority let not the wife speak against the husband as though she would usurp authority over him. The unmarried should honor Christ in their individual lives, but the married also in their married lives. So the Lord is the spirit of the letter in Gen. ii. 18–24, and when that is recognized and realized, there will come spiritual life to the married state.

No unmarried man is the head of any woman. If one thinks differently let him try to exercise his authority over the first woman he meets and see if "nature itself" (in the woman) don't teach him the error of his conceit. Here our Revision needs revising. When this is done woman will have the latitude and longitude that God gave her, but which has been taken away by an erroneous translation. Neither the law nor the gospel subjects the woman to the man, but only the wife to the husband. This is both the letter and the spirit of Gen. ii. 18-24 and like Scriptures. See also Num. xxx; 1 Cor. xi. 3; xiv. 34, 35; Eph. v. 22–33; 1 Tim. ii. 11–15; Titus ii. 3–5; 1 Peter iii. 1–7.

Chapter V.

On the same principle of spiritual interpretation I see in the institution of the Sabbath (Gen. ii. 1–3) not only a literal seventh day of rest, but also a greater spiritual millennial day of rest, "for the people of God." (Heb. iv. 5–11). This typical day of rest was not fulfilled by the rest in Canaan, the promised land; for if Joshua had led the people into the antitypical rest, David would not have written of it in after centuries as still unattained. Nor would the writer of the Hebrews have concluded that it was still future and yet to be attained. I believe the six days of labor will soon close, and that the long promised rest will soon be realized by those who "do not come short of it." "Let us therefore earnestly endeavor to enter into that rest, that no one may fall after the same example of disbelief." When we keep it, not according to the oldness of the letter, but according to the newness of the spirit, we show retrospectively that God rested from his labors on the seventh day, and prospectively, that on a seventh day "there remains a Sabbath rest for the people of God." As Jehovah God kept it with man in the type, so will Jehovah Jesus keep it with man in the antitype. As in the type there was no sin and Satan to molest, so in the antitype Satan will be bound and paradise restored. (Rev. xx). How uplifting and life-giving is such an observance! How burdensome the letter (only) that kills; how delightful the Spirit (also) that makes alive. "Remember the Sabbath day to keep it holy." Cease from your six days of labor. Look back at Jehovah resting with man in the beautiful juvenile earth. Look forward to Jehovah resting with man in a rebeautified and rejuvenated earth.

"That better day is coming, that morning promised long,
When girded Right, with holy Might, will overthrow the wrong,
When God the Lord will listen to every plaintive sigh,
And stretch his hand o'er every land in justice by and by.

The boast of haughty Error no more will fill the air,

But Age and Youth will love the truth, and spread it every-
    where;
No more from saints and Martyrs will come the hopeless cry;
For wars will cease, and perfect peace will flourish by and by.

Oh! for that holy dawning we watch and wait and pray;
Till o'er the height the morning light shall drive the gloom
    away;
And when the heavenly glory shall flood the earth and sky,
We'll bless the Lord for all his Word, we'll see him by and by."

"We shall not always labor, we shall not always cry;
The end is drawing nearer, the end for which we sigh;
We'll lay these heavy burdens down, and rest us by and by."

Thus we may keep the Sabbath not in oldness of letter (only), but (also) in newness of spirit. Unless the vail is lifted from the mind and heart and Scripture, we will not see "the Lord the Spirit" in the ordinance of the holy Sabbath. The letter only is burdensome, but the Spirit makes it delightsome.

The third chapter of Genesis gives an account of the temptation and the fall. Can we not find "the Lord the Spirit" in that narrative? Not in all the details of it, but in the heart of it. The Lord was in the temple, not in the nails and curtains and other minutiae; but in the sacrifices of the outer court, the blood and shewbread and candlestick of the inner court, and in the High Priest, ark, and shekinah of the Holy of Holies. The other things were but helps and pointers directing the "comers" to where the Lord was revealed. So all parables and figures and types and narratives have their curtains and fringes and ornaments to decorate the place and person of the revealed Lord. In the old Scriptures, let the Lord be recognized in every appellation of the Father, for he was with the Father before the beginning, in the beginning and from the beginning.

But especially note that "Christ manifest in the flesh" is revealed in the promised seed of the woman. (Read also Isa. vii. 14; Mic. v. 2, 3; Matt. i. 22–25; Luke i. 31–35; Gal. iv. 4). According to one's faith and power to interpret, let him also, if he can, discern "the Lord the Spirit," in Adam taking upon him the fallen state of his wife, as Christ took upon himself our sins (Rom. v. 12–19); also in the "skins" of the sacrifices, which sacrifices pointed to the Lamb of God; also in the flaming sword which turned every way to keep the tree of life; also in the exclamation of Eve: "I have gotten a man from the Lord;" or as some think—I have gotten a man, even Jehovah; uttered in her haste to realize the fulfillment of the promised seed, which is here in the singular number, and referred to by Paul in Gal. iii. 16.* The same promised seed was reiterated to Abraham, and was to come in the line of Abraham (Gen. xxii.

[* I have before me a wonderful book—"The Memorial Name," by Alex. Mac Whorter, and Introduction by N. W. Taylor, both of Yale. (Gould & Lincoln, Boston). He shows that Jehovah, translated Lord, is from Yahveh, and that Ex. iii. 14-15—I am that I am, I am hath sent me unto you—should read: I Will Be Who I Will Be; I who will be hath sent me unto you, etc. He says on page 23: "With respect to the exegesis of the term Jehovah, so far as the interest of criticism is concerned, all scholars are now agreed." He says on page 31: "It was natural that Eve should expect to witness in her lifetime the realization of the promise. Filled with this expectation, it was natural that, looking upon her first-born, she should exclaim: 'I have received Him, even Yahveh'—'even He

18 Sept), of Isaac (Gen. xxi. 12 Sept; Rom. ix. 7), and of David (Ps. cxxxii. 11; Luke i. 69; Acts ii. 30). This seed referred primarily to Christ, and secondarily to the children God gave him (Heb. ii. 13-18). Through Christ primarily, and the seeds (plural)—the spiritual children of Abraham, God had promised to bless all the nations of the earth. When Christ (Luke xxiv. 27) began at Moses and all the prophets, and expounded unto them in all the Scriptures the things concerning himself, showing that it behooved him according to the old Scriptures to suffer these things and to enter into his glory, who can doubt that he expounded the Scriptures in a way similar to the inspired exposition given in Hebrews; revealing himself in unexpected places, especially expounding the sacrifices as typical of his sacrifice. If so, may he not have gone back in Moses to the third chapter of Genesis, to the sacrifice that Adam

---

Who Will Be !'—and that she should have believed him the promised Deliverer. That she did so believe, the record, literally interpreted, leaves no room to doubt." On page 30 he says this name, Yahveh, is a proclamation, a promise, and a prophecy of Christ; that it represented the expectation of the world: that this expectation of a Deliverer finds its source in the First Great Promise or Prediction, that the Seed of the woman shall bruise the Serpent's head; that it was applied by Eve to her first-born—transferred to God—invoked by the Patriarchs—affirmed by Moses—proclaimed by the Prophets—complete in Christ."

I add this suggestion. If the name was delivered to us in the Christ or Messiah, is not the idea of Yahveh still retained? True, he came in the flesh, but is he not yet to come in the glory of the Father? Did not his first coming assure us of his second? Is he not to us He Who Will Come? For yet a very little while, the Coming One will come, and will not delay.—Heb. 10:37.]

made, and to the skins of those sacrifices with which he hid his nakedness, and to the excellent sacrifice of Heb. xi. 4. Is it not right for us to search what, or what manner of time the Spirit of Christ which was in the prophets did signify, when it testified beforehand the sufferings of Christ and the glory that should follow? (1 Peter ii. 11).

I am afraid that some will stop their ears and turn away from the truth, because such interpretation as this is "fanciful." It may not be in many particulars correct in application, but that this principle of interpretation is correct will be shown by much that is to follow, and which cannot be gainsaid, because inspired. But I must strive at brevity or I will write a book on the first division—the Letter and Spirit. I can only tap the Scriptures here and there, but I will try to do it at safe and sure places, so as to invite and not divert attention and interest. In Gen. ix. 6 and Jas. iii. 9 I would call attention to the Spirit of the letter. "Whoso sheddeth man's blood, by man shall his blood be shed; for in the image of God made he man." "Therewith bless we God even the Father; and therewith curse we men which are made after the similitude of God."

The law—"Thou shalt not kill," and thou shalt not injure thy neighbor—may be kept in letter and not in Spirit. I may refrain from killing and cursing a man through fear of the law, and thus keep it in letter. But "the law is also Spiritual" and "the Lord is that Spirit." So when I regard man as in

Abel, by which he obtained witness that he was righteous, and by which he being dead yet speaketh, the likeness of Christ, and Christ as the image of God (Heb. i. 3), and refrain from violence because of that fact, then I keep that law with respect to God, and I respect and reverence my fellow-man because he bears the divine image. A man that kills his fellow-man ought not to live, "For in the image of God made he man." Obedience is Spiritual when it is Christ-ward, God-ward. By the Spirit, through the Son, unto the Father (Eph. ii. 18). Whether we eat or drink or whatsoever we do, let us do it to the glory of God. Let us cultivate this Spirit of obedience until it reaches to the minutest details of life, even to the "Whatsoever."

Chapter VI.

I recommend, yea, I insist, that you study the works on Typology. This will assist very much in the development of this way of interpreting the Scriptures. These works may not always be correct in their exposition, explanation and application. But what works of man are free from errors in these things? We must not disdain a mine because it is not all gold, but seek diligently for the little gold there is in it. The danger with young preachers is that they will think lightly of types and shadows because they do not know how to understand them. God adapted his teaching to the ignorance of the people by addressing their minds through the eye as well as the ear—their accustomed way of learning. Agabus the prophet made his exhortation to Paul more impressive by taking Paul's girdle and binding his own hands and feet, and then said: "Thus shall the Jews at Jerusalem bind the man that owns this girdle." (Acts xi. 28; xxi. 11). So when God would teach the ignorant Jews that their sins must be imputed to one without sin, and that he must put them away by the sacrifice of the sinbearer, he appoints the lamb without blemish, and through its bloody and fiery sacrifice they could see Jesus, the lamb of God that should take away the sins of the world. And when God would teach the great doctrine of atonement he appointed two goats, one to bear their sins into death, and so fulfill the law—"The soul that sins shall die;" the other to bear their sins into an uninhabited wilderness, to remind them that when sins were remitted by the shedding of blood, they were also put away as far as the East is from the West, never to come up in remembrance against them any more forever. Thus sins are not only expiated in law and in the mind of God, but they were also taken away from the conscience. That this is not a myth, but a mighty reality, I ask you about those sins that were made alive in your conscience when under conviction, and which gave you sorrow and trouble of soul. When God heard your prayer for mercy and forgave your sins, was it simply a matter that pertained to God's mind, or did he not also scapegoat your sins—send them away from your consciences, so that they "left" you, and "let you alone?" And is not the word translated forgive also translated left, and let alone, i. e., left you and let you alone? Have those forgiven sins ever come back into your consciences and troubled you again? If forgiveness is only in the mind of God, how could the people in Christ's day know that he had power on earth to forgive or scapegoat sins? How else could David assure himself of sins forgiven? If the Bible were nothing but letter; if it had only the natural and historical meanings about these goats, well might infidels laugh it to scorn. But when we put "The Lord the Spirit" into the letter, and then test its meaning by our experience and conscience, then we have knowledge, yea, conscious knowledge. Then we can say:

> "This precious book I'd rather own,
>   Than all the gold and gems
> That e'er in monarch's coffers shone—
>   Than all their diadems.
> Nay, were the seas one chrysolite,
>   The earth a golden ball,
> And diamonds all the stars of night,
>   This book were worth them all.
>
> No, no, the soul ne'er found relief
>   In glittering hoards of wealth;
> Gems dazzle not the eye of grief;
>   Gold cannot purchase health.
> But here a blessed balm appears,
>   To heal the deepest woe;
> And he that seeks this book in tears,
>   His tears shall cease to flow.
>
> Yes, yes, this precious book is worth
>   All else to mortals given—
> For what are all the joys of earth
>   Compared to joys of heaven?
> This is the guide our Father gave,
>   To lead to realms of day;
> A star whose lustre gilds the grave—
>   "'The Light—the Life—the way.'"

If there was not Spirit as well as letter, and if the Lord was not that Spirit, the Bible would be like other books. Now let me insist that you turn to Gen. xvi. to xxi. and read about Sarah and Hagar and Ishmael and Isaac, and then turn to Gal. iv. 21-31 and read an inspired comment on it. If this way of interpreting Scripture is fanciful, as many have charged, then Paul and the Holy Spirit are guilty. So read of the food the Israelites ate in Ex. xvi. 15, 35; Neh. ix. 15, 20, and Psa. lxxviii. 24. Then read of the water out of the smitten rock in Ex. xvii. 6; Num. xx. 11; Psa. lxxviii. 15, and turning to 1 Cor. x. 3-4 Paul calls it " Spiritual meat and Spiritual drink," and said " that Rock was Christ." Is that fanciful? Here were both Letter and Spirit. Those who ate the literal bread died, and those who drank the literal water died. But there was a Spirit in this letter, and that Spirit was Christ. The Spirit of that manna-bread that was given from heaven testified of the true bread that should come down from heaven, of which one might eat and live forever. The one sustained the body for a while, the other sustains the soul forever. The literal water quenched the thirst of the body for a while; the Spiritual water quenches the thirst of the soul forever. Is this fanciful? Can it be verified? Can not all of you testify that as surely as you have experienced that natural bread and water give satisfaction to the body, so surely do " the Spiritual meat and drink" give satisfaction to the spirit of man that is in you? When Christ and the Scriptures call thirsting souls to the water of life that they may drink, can they not go and drink and live and testify that the promise and fulfillment are everlasting realities? If these Spiritual things are not real, and to be realized, then indeed is the whole matter fanciful and deceitful. The natural man who has not realized these Spiritual truths, and yet tries to be religious, has supplanted them with divers lotions and diluted potions composed of rites and compounded of ritual. "Having the form but denying the power." An unbitten Israelite could gaze at the brazen serpent, yea, handle it with his hands, and it would do him no good. So an unconvicted sinner could see Christ and dwell with him and handle him and in externals obey him; yea, could have the real blood of Christ sprinkled profusely on him; yea, poured on him; yea, immersed in it as was Joseph's coat in the blood of the kid; yea, with the mouth could profess to love him and confirm it with a shower of kisses, as Judas did, and it all might be the Letter that kills. But if a bitten and swollen and burning Israelite could look at the brazen serpent on the pole, and "when he looked he lived," so a sinner convicted of the Holy Spirit and dying of spiritual hunger and thirst, can look with the eye of faith to Christ on the cross as God's remedy for sin, and "when he looks he lives." If this is not a Spiritual reality, and if you have not realized it, then to you having not Spiritual discernment and experience it is all a myth, a fable, yea, an old wive's fable. May all eyes be made to see and all hearts to understand these Spiritual things.

Chapter VII.

I am afraid that you will weary with this if I continue it further. It will not be necessary to continue the investigation of the other two divisions of this subject to such lengths. The Bible is the storehouse of the spiritual provisions for the "Spiritual Man," and the directory of The "Spiritual Religion" we are next to discuss, and it requires more time and attention than either or perhaps both of the other subjects. So let us open another door and make another appropriation from this store-house of spiritual food. The key that opens this door is in Rom. xv. 4: "For whatsoever things were written in former times were written for our instruction, that we through patience and through consolation of the Scriptures may have hope." Westcott and Hort read: "All things whatsoever." That is more than we know how to appropriate, and more than we can appropriate. But let us help ourselves freely to a little more of it. If the tense is Perfect, as is generally the case, in speaking of the act of writing, it holds a connection with the present, and shows the "things written" have an abiding and permanent consequence. Or, if the tense be Aorist, as in the above and in Rom. iv. 23 and 1 Cor. x. 11, which are presently to be noticed, the tense would cal attention to the act of writing, as though the inspired writer took his pen, not simply to write something of permanent interest, and of which all might partake, but the astonishing idea is that he took his pen to write especially to us, that is, to us of any subsequent time, as the Aorist has no limit, that while he was writing of, something or some one in the then present or past, yet he was writing it especially for those of the future. Apply this to the case of Abraham, whose faith and justification Paul was discussing at length in the 4th chapter of Romans. What sort of faith justified Abraham? Do you ask what is that to us, as Abraham lived in a former and different administration? Much to us every way. Paul in quoting the things Moses wrote of Abraham declares that Moses did not write those things for Abraham's sake alone, or as mere historical facts to the memory of Abraham, for Abraham was dead when Moses wrote them, but Moses wrote to us, telling us how God justified Abraham that we might know that God would justify us in the same way. Not simply permitting us to know, but he wrote that we might know.

So here is a double meaning in Scripture, containing not only the literal history of Abraham, but ourselves are included. Written by Moses for our sakes that we through comfort of the Scriptures might have hope. If written for Abraham's sake alone then to us the Scriptures would be a dead letter, worth no more than any other history, if indeed as much. We may learn how to be great by reading the history of great men, but we could not learn how to be justified by reading this history of Abraham, if God has changed his way of justification. The different ways would confuse us and mislead us. "All things whatsoever written aforetime" were written not only for our learning, but that we might have hope. Christ states it thus to the Jews: "Search the Scriptures, for in them ye think ye have eternal life: And they are they which testify of me." "For if ye believed Moses ye would believe me; for he wrote of me. But if ye believe not his writings, how shall ye believe my words?" (Jno. v. 39, 46, 47). Now read verse 40: "And ye will not come to me that ye might have life." This means that the old Scriptures were sufficient for salvation, and not only so, but sufficient to show the way of salvation. Ye will not come to me (according to the old Scriptures) that ye might have life. When Dives petitioned Abraham, both of them in the spirit world, where there is more knowledge than here, to send a preacher to his five brethren to keep them from coming to his place of torment, Abraham's answer was: "They have Moses and the prophets, let them hear them." When Dives insisted that one from the dead would be more effective, the reply was: "If they hear not Moses and the prophets, neither would they be persuaded though one rose from the dead." The Living Oracles of God, that is, the old Scriptures, are more potent as means of salvatiou than the ministry even of resurrected saints would be. By a transfiguration tableau, the three choice disciples were made eye witnesses of the majesty and glory of Christ's second coming; and not only eye witnesses, but ear witnesses, for they not only heard a voice, but such a voice; and he repeats, " this voice we heard," and this glory we saw, and this power we felt; yet the word of prophecy is " more sure" than this tripple testimony of these select men. And not only so, but the testimony of the prophets was more sure to the witnesses themselves than their own vision in the holy mount, for Peter says: "We have," and that includes himself. So he exhorts others to give more heed to the prophets than to their testimony, though that was as strong as human testimony could be. Three witnesses, specially favored to see Christ transfigured to his second coming, and yet Christ's second coming is more plainly taught by the prophets of the old Scriptures. So we ought to give more earnest heed to these Scriptures, "as unto a light shining in a dark place (and will shine) until the day dawn and the day star arise in our hearts. There is more in them than the literal meaning. Abraham had no Scriptures, and yet he was taught of God by signs and symbols, and in those signs and symbols he rejoiced to see Christ's day, and he saw it, and was glad. (Jno. viii. 56).

Peter on the day of Pentecost referred to Ps. xvi. 8-10 in a way that showed his deep spiritual insight. If you have never compared the old Scriptures with their quotations by the apostle, by all means begin it. Study this one in parallel columns for an example:

Psalms xvi.	Acts ii.
8 I have set the Lord always before me; because *he is* at my right hand, I shall not be moved. 9 Therefore my heart is glad, and my glory rejoiceth: my flesh also shall rest in hope. 10 For thou wilt not leave my soul in hades; nither wilt thou suffer thine Holy One to see corruption. 11 Thou wilt shew me the path of life: in thy presence *is* fulness of joy; at thy right hand *there are* pleasures for evermore.	25 For David speaketh concerning him, I forsaw the Lord always before my face; for he is on my right hand, that I should not be moved: 26 Therefore did my heart rejoice, and my tongue was glad; moreover also my flesh shall rest in hope: 27 Because thou wilt not leave my soul in hades, neither wilt thou suffer thine Holy One to see corruption. Thou hast made known to me the ways of life; thou shalt make me full of joy with their presence.

Paul quotes this Psalm in Acts xiii. 34–37, and he also makes it apply to Christ. Both Peter and Paul make the application, not to David, but to Christ. Then does it not follow that the whole Psalm is Messianic, as there is but one speaker from first to last? Then does it not follow that there is more of Christ in that Psalm than has commonly been recognized? Then may it not be so with other Psalms? Then may it not be so with all the Scriptures? As Christ says of the old Scriptures in general, "They are they which testify of me." Were not all the converts before and on Pentecost, and even after (from the Jews), made by preaching Christ out of the old Scriptures? Examine the following: Acts iii. 22–26, where Deut. xviii. 15, 19 is quoted and applied to Christ. Also other prophecies; and Acts iv. 4 shows the result: "Howbeit many of them that heard the word believed, and the number of the men was about five thousand." Stephen asks in Acts vii. 52: "Which of the prophets have not your fathers persecuted? And they slew them which showed before of the coming of the Just One." Here is a good text for you young preachers. Search the prophets, and show who, and where, and how they showed before the coming of the Just One. Several such texts may be found in Luke xxiv. 25–47. Especially would I recommend 1 Cor. xv. 3, 4. Did not Philip begin at Isa. liii. and preach Christ unto the Ethiopian? Did not Peter in Acts x. 43 prove the way of salvation by the prophets? "To Him give all the prophets witness, that through his name whosoever believeth in him should receive remission of sins." See also Acts xiii. 5, 29, 44–49, where the old Scriptures as the word of the Lord was glorified and the result was—"as many as were ordained to eternal life believed." Examine closely also the following. Give these passages some peculiar mark so you can read them consecutively: Acts xvii. 4, 11–13; xviii. 4, 11, 24–28; xxiv. 14–16; xxvi. 22, 23, 27, 28; xxviii. 23, 24. Also in the Gospels where it says, "This was done that it might be fulfilled;" and also in the Epistles where the old Scriptures are quoted in proof of "New Testament doctrines," so called. The first eleven chapters of Romans abound with such quotations. So Galatians, and all the doctrinal letters of the apostolic writings—especially the Hebrews. And don't overlook 2 Tim. iii. 15–17. Timothy when a child didn't know a word of the New Testament, for it was not then written, nor any part of it, if dates are right. And yet Paul says the Scriptures his mother and grandmother taught him were "able to make him wise unto salvation through faith in Christ," and that they were profitable for doctrine, and sufficient for all good works.

As a conclusion from all this I would impress you that there is more in the old Scriptures than appears on the surface. Unspiritual men are literalizing and criticising the inspired or inbreathed thought of God out of the Scriptures, and these teachers are so popular that some of you may want a few lessons in their destructive criticisms. I want no man to teach me the Scriptures who teaches that way. They are the spiritually unlearned and unstable who "wrest the Scriptures unto their own destruction."

Before closing this subject let us make another draw or two from the wonderful Book. See how Paul in 1 Cor. ix. 9–11 drew an argument for Ministerial support, from Deut. xxv. 4: "For it is written in the law of Moses, Thou shalt not muzzle the mouth of the ox that treadeth out the corn. Doth God take care for oxen? Or saith he it altogether for our sakes? For our sakes, no doubt, this is written: that he that plougheth should plow in hope; and that he that thresheth in hope should be partaker of his hope. If we have sown unto you spiritual things, is it a great thing if we shall reap your carnal things?" See also in verses 13 and 14 how he appropriates Lev. vi. 16, 26: "Do ye not know that they which minister about holy things live of the things of the temple? and they which wait at the altar are partakers with the altar? Even so hath the Lord ordained that they which preach the gospel should live of the gospel." See also in 1 Cor. x. 6-12 how he uses the example found in Num. xiv.: "Now these things were our examples, to the intent we should not lust after evil things, as they also lusted. Neither be ye idolaters, as were some of them; as it is written, The people sat down to eat and drink, and rose up to play. Neither let us commit fornication, as some of them committed, and fell in one day three and twenty thousand. Neither let us tempt Christ, as some of them also tempted, and were destroyed of serpents. Neither murmur ye, as some of them also murmured, and were destroyed of the destroyer. Now all these things happened unto them for ensamples: and they are written for our admonition, upon whom the ends of the world are come."

Now if all things whatsoever were written in the old Scriptures were written for our learning and warning and consolation and hope (Rom. xv. 4), and if according to verse 11 above those things happened to them for examples, and that they were written (Aorist) for our admonition, upon whom the ends of the world are come, then the old Scriptures are Living Oracles (Acts vii. 38), and not the dead letter of a past dispensation of works or grace. Yet thousands feel they are called to teach that the old Scriptures and the four Gospels are the dead oracles of God. Mr. A. Campbell called his translation of the New Testament " Living Oracles." This title he borrowed from Acts vii. 38, but he butchered the text from which he borrowed, for that calls the old Scriptures Living Oracles. His disciples generally, as far as I know, follow their leader in this disparagement of the old Scriptures and the four Gospels, and even the first chapter of Acts. It is also asserted that the way of salvation can't be learned even from the Epistles. See "Proper Division of the Word of God," by E. G. Sewell, pp. 8, 9, 11, 12; also "Acts of Apostles," by same author, pp. 3, 7, 13, 14, 15, 21, 22; also "Peculiarities of the Disciples," by B. B. Tyler, pp. 44, 45, 48, 49; also their literature generally. This shows the importance of magnifying the old Scriptures as " the Word of God that lives and abides forever," and which are as much for our good as for those in the past dispensation. Not the Letter but the Spirit is for us. And the Lord is that Spirit.

THE NATURAL AND THE SPIRITUAL.

CHAPTER VIII.

We have tried so far to discern somewhat between the Letter and the Spirit of the Scriptures. Thus God provided for the Natural and Spiritual Man—the Letter for the Natural and the Spirit for the Spiritual Man. By Letter I do not mean verbal inspiration. I believe in verbal inspiration, not of translations, but of the original writings. By Letter and Spirit I mean that the verbal inspiration is susceptible of two meanings—the natural, literal, personal and historical, which the natural man can understand. In addition to this, there is a spiritual meaning, which only the spiritual man can discern, and this must be spiritually discerned. The spiritual man has natural and intellectual discernment, and he may exercise himself only as a natural man in discerning. He should aim to exercise himself also in spiritual discernment. Indeed, the natural man may have an intellectual discernment of spiritual things, and may have an exercise of his emotions in so doing. Emotions and intellections belong to the natural man. But the new man—the new-born man, the newly created man—has in addition, a new nature, and this new nature has new perceptions and emotions and experiences. Natural

Jews ate "spiritual meat" and "drank spiritual drink" (1 Cor. x. 2, 3), but they did not spiritually discern, and therefore did not eat and drink spiritually, and they got no life out of the life-giving food and drink. Indeed, a spiritual Jew may have gone through the same performances with the same results. If the spiritual man eats the bread and drinks the wine of the Lord's Supper, not discerning (spiritually) the Lord's body and blood, broken and shed for him, he eats and drinks condemnation to himself. Why? Not because he is not spiritual, nor because the emblems are not spiritual, but because he did not eat and drink spiritually. The "unworthily" qualifies the act. "The fire will try every man's work of what sort it is." We never can preserve a Regenerated Church Membership unless we learn to discern between the natural and the spiritual man, and not only so, but also between Formal and Spiritual Religion. We should examine both ourselves and others lest there should be deception about natural and spiritual things.

As to discerning this difference in the Scriptures, I have only written a preface. Not a preface of what I shall hereafter write, but a preface, I trust, to what others may write. This is a new way of treating the subject, as far as I know. If I can prepare the way for others who will continue the instruction, I will have performed a good work.

Now let us begin the second division of the subject, The Natural and the Spiritual in Man. There are several Scriptures to be used, but let us begin with 1 Cor. ii. 14: "But a natural man receives not the things of the Spirit of God, for they are foolishness to him, neither can he know them, because they are spiritually discerned." Be sure to read from chapter i. 18 to iv. 5, and you will get the body of which the text quoted is the heart and soul. That which is born of the flesh is flesh (natural man), and that which is born of the Spirit is Spirit. Hence birth of the Spirit is necessary to "see" or "discern" spiritual things. Thus we conclude that saints possess a dual nature—all that belongs to the natural man, plus something called Spirit—(that which is born of the Spirit is Spirit). After the resurrection the saints will be spiritual even as to their bodies. It is sown a natural body, that is, it is a natural body till death; then in the resurrection it will be raised a spiritual body, and will be like Christ and the angels, not subject to natural law. Till death the regenerated man is both natural and spiritual. This is often overlooked. The old man is influenced by the new man, but the old and the new live together in the same house, the body. They don't always get along very well together. Indeed, they war with each other. The dual man fights a duel, and both at times suffer defeat.

The natural man with his mind discerns natural things, and with his soul discerns moral things. The spiritual man continues with these self-same discerning faculties, with one added, namely, the spirit to discern spiritual things. As ong as the spiritual man is related to natural things, he must retain his natural faculties. Don't forget that the moral belongs to the natural. The most moral men that ever lived were natural men. Their religion consisted of morality, and hence they were moralists, and it was to this very class that Christ put the question, "How shall ye escape the damnation of hell?" Here is where regenerated church membership suffers. If a man has a decent moral character we take him in and hold him in full fellowship. If he is strict about the observance of the Sabbath and sobriety and honesty and the forms of religion, he is above suspicion. Of course his morals must be right, but unless he has more than good morals he is not fit for the kingdom of God. We can't maintain spiritual church membership with moralists, and certainly not with immoral men. Hence in discerning between the natural and the spiritual we must discern between the moral and the spiritual. "The law was given through Moses; grace and truth came through Jesus Christ" (Jno. i. 17). This does not mean that there was no law till Moses and no grace and truth till Christ came. Far from it. The law has poured out its blessings and curses from the fall of man, and streams of grace and truth have poured from Jesus Christ during the same time. (Send ten cents for three tracts by the writer, developing these thoughts further than he can now do). The meaning is, that through Moses and Christ were given the expressions of law and grace. The law in its letter is for natural men, and they can discern it sufficiently to get a knowledge of sin and a just condemnation, and hence their need of a Savior. That is what law is for, and if morality were sufficient, Moses would be a sufficient Savior. The law is also spiritual, but the spirituality of the law is not discerned by the natural man, nor can it be.

The race of man died in Adam. (Rom. v. 12; 2 Cor. v. 14). Not intellectually or morally, but spiritually. The whole race died spiritually the day Adam sinned; that is, died to God, so that God was feared and not desired. The heart with its affections became estranged from God, and his mind became enmity against God. Regeneration is begetting again of these lost affections, and Religion is binding again to God. The church is to be composed of those who have been thus restored. Before the fall Adam enjoyed God's presence. After the fall he hid. Joy turned to fear and shame and terror; and this was entailed on his posterity. All by nature love sin and hate holiness. This is a FACT. I don't mean hate that which is natural, including the social and moral and intellectual, but hate holiness, that essential character of God on account of which he cannot and will not tolerate sin. When man is begotten of God, or is bound back to God, he becomes partaker of the Divine nature—God-like, loving and hating what God loves and hates. In receiving members into the cnurch, this is the main point of enquiry. Let the candidate assure himself and the church that he is dead in his love to sin and has become alive in his love of holiness—the opposite of sin—loving what he once hated and hating what he once loved. Don't ask him if he is born of God, but enquire after the fruits of the new birth. Christ told Nicodemus about the new birth as plainly as it can be told, and even Nicodemus could not understand it. That ought to suffice for all time, and no doubt was intended for that. The natural man can't discern the spiritual birth, yet grace has provided for him to receive it. While it is a fact that the natural man loves sin, there is another fact as indisputable, and that is, regeneration reverses this. There are multiplied millions of witnesses to this whose lives verify the truth. Saul of Tarsus is only one witness. I am another, and I can speak for many others, though some must speak for themselves.

To excite thought, and I trust investigation, let me say here that regeneration is the Spirit's work, while salvation is Christ's work. Regeneration is never ascribed to Christ, nor is salvation ever ascribed to the Spirit. The Father, Son and Spirit are co-workers in man's salvation, each performing his part. If regeneration or a restoration to our forfeited relations to God were all, the regenerated might fall, as Adam, with much better surroundings, fell from his holy state. Regenerated men in some way sin and need more than regeneration; so there have been brought in Redemption from the law principle of life; also forgiveness of sins, sanctification, justification, adoption, preservation, resurrection and final glorification. This is the work of the triune God, and so sacred is this unity in co-operation that I would not presume to pry into close discriminations. But may we not say that in a prominent way the Spirit regenerates, Christ saves and God the Father justifies or condemns? So that the church should be composed of those having both qualifications, viz., regeneration and salvation. The Lord added the saved to the church.

And let me here point out a difference between forgiveness and justification. The law is both prohibitory and preceptive, telling us what we must not do and also what we must do. If we do the things we should not, we are sinners. If we do not the things we should do, we are unrighteous. Forgiveness takes away the sins and makes us innocent. Justification imputes the obedience of Christ and makes us righteous. If one goes fifty miles in the wrong direction, forgiveness would put him back where he started. But he ought to have been fifty miles in the opposite direction. Justification puts him there. In general parlance, justification is swallowed up of forgiveness and forgiveness is swallowed up of pardon, a term not found in the new version, and ought not to be found in the old. The governor may pardon a criminal at the expense of justice, but God don't deal that way with sinners. He either justifies or condemns. If he justifies he forgives by making a righteous disposition of his sins. Some one must bear them and answer for them. Christ stands for the two goats which give perfect satisfaction, one to the law and the other to the conscience. After putting sins completely away, God justifies by imputing the righteousness of Christ. It appears to me to be a travesty, if not sacrilege, to associate such a great transaction with the popular and contemptible practice of pardon. In my petitions I never use the term pardon. Christ is not the end of law for pardon, nor did Pal say, Therefore being pardoned by faith let us haxe peace with God. Pardon is always unjust. If the prisoner is not guilty he doesn't need pardon, but acquittal. If he is guilty he deserves the punishment, and pardon is a release from a part or all of the punishment, and of course is unjust. But God is always just when he justifies the ungodly. He makes no allowanc for the sin, but treats it vicariously, and he who takes our sins upon himself makes full satisfaction both to the law of God and to the conscience of the sinner.

I make this seeming digression in order to mag nify the material for the temple of God. Not sin ners "desiring to flee from the wrath to come" and join the church as a shelter from the coming wrath. Not sinners who through fear of hell would amend their lives and join the church to get better associa tions and facilities. What a cage of unclean birds is such a so-called church. A regenerated church membership means also the saved, and that means redeemed, sanctified, justified, etc. Paul addressing a church of Christ says: "Such were some of you, but ye were washed, but ye were sanctified, but ye were justified in the name of the Lord Jesus Christ, and in the Spirit of our God" (1 Cor. vi. 11); and they did not get this in the church, but before joining it. Christ is the door into the sheepfold. If any one enter in through him he shall be saved. But if he enters not through this door into the sheepfold, but climbs up some other way, he is a thief and a robber. (Jno. x. 1, 7-10). Mark, he who goes in through Christ shall be saved. If he goes in through baptism and promises of repentance he is a thief and a robber. See Methodist Discipline (1883), pp. 28-33, 243-246 for a perversion of "the way, the truth and the life." Study it, and learn by it to shun such a way, and hold up to sinners "Christ before the church" and before baptism and before the good works the Discipline describes. Thus you may have regenerated church membership and spiritual worship.

CHAPTER IX.

Before making further remarks on the Dual nature of the Regenerate man, let us get some of the Scriptures before us sustaining this doctrine. "For he is not a Jew who is one outwardly, nor is that cricumcision which is outward in the flesh. But he is a Jew who is one inwardly; and circumcision is that of the heart, in spirit, not in letter; whose praise is not of men, but of God." (Rom. ii. 28, 29). This difference between a natural Jew and a spiritual Jew was effected by the New Covenant. Let every preacher familiarize himself with the frequent references and statements of the New Covenant, which began its operations when the first soul was regenerated. These references in part are as follows: Jer. xxxi. 31–34; xxxii. 38–40; Ez. xi. 19, 20; xxxvi. 25–28; Heb. viii. 6–13; x. 16, 17. The same inward divine operation that converted a natural Jew into a spiritual Jew is necessary to convert a natural Gentile into a spiritual Gentile. This constitutes the new birth that all must have to discern and enjoy spiritual life and light. "That which is born of the flesh is flesh, and that which is born of the Spirit is Spirit," is a succinct statement of the whole quesfion. The new part of the regenerated man called "the inner man" and "the hidden man of the heart" is sometimes put for the whole man. "Whosoever believeth that Jesus is the Christ has been begotten of God," and "Whosoever is begotten of God sinneth not," are examples of the new man being put for the whole man. But sometimes the two parts of the dual man are referred to separately. "Put off as concerns your former conduct the old man, . . . put on the new man who was created after God in rightecusness and holiness of truth." (Eph. iv. 22-24). Also Col. iii. 9, 10: "Seeing ye have put off the old man with his deeds, and have put on the new man, who is being renewed in knowledge according to the image of him who created him." Also in Eph. iii. 16: "Strengthened with might in the inner man." Also 2 Cor. iv. 16: "Wherefore we faint not; but though our outward man is decaying, yet our inward man is renewed day by day." Also Gal. v. 16, 17: "Walk by the Spirit, and ye will not fulfil the desire of the flesh. For the flesh has desires against the Spirit, and the Spirit against the flesh; and these are contrary the one to the other, that ye may not do those things that ye wish." I entertain some doubt as to whether Spirit in the above and in the first seventeen verses of the 8th chapter of Romans should be capitalized except where "the Spirit of Christ," "of God," "of him," or "his Spirit" is mentioned. Translators differ. The Oxford Revision differs from the one we quote from, viz., Broadus, Hovey and Weston. Here I like the Oxford better. The Spirit not being capitalized in the Greek, it is often left to human wisdom to decide whether the Holy Spirit is referred to or the spirit that is in man. If we should walk by our spirit instead of our flesh, or the new man instead of the old, it is on the principle that the "Holy Spirit testifies with our spirit," and by Him our spirit is taught and strengthened and impressed and led; so the difference is not so very great. But study the following quotation especially from both standpoints as capitalized in the Oxford and Broadus, Hovey and Weston:

Rom. viii. 4-17: " That the requirement of the law might be fulfilled in us, who walk not according to the flesh, but according to the Spirit. For they that are according to the flesh mind the things of the flesh; but they that are according to the Spirit, the things of the Spirit. For the mind of the flesh is death; but the mind of the Spirit is life and peace. Because the mind of the flesh is enmity against God; for it does not subject itself to the law of God, neither indeed can it; and they that are in the flesh can not please God. But ye are not in the flesh, but in the Spirit, if indeed the Spirit of God dwells in you. And if any one has not the Spirit of Christ, he is none of his. And if Christ is in you, the body is dead because of sin; but the Spirit is life because of righteousness. And if the Spirit of him who raised Jesus from the dead dwells in you, he who raised Christ from the dead will make alive your mortal bodies also, because of his Spirit that dwells in you. So then, brethren, we are debtors, not to the flesh, to live according to the flesh. For if ye are living according to the flesh, ye are going to die; but if by the Spirit ye put to death the deeds of the body, ye will live. For as many as are led by the Spirit of God, these are sons of God. For ye did not receive a spirit of bondage again unto fear; but ye received a spirit of adoption, whereby we cry, Abba, Father.

The Spirit himself testifies with our spirit that we are children of God; and if children, also heirs; heirs of God, and joint heirs with Christ, if indeed we suffer with him, that we may also be glorified with him."

In the above, spirit occurs sixteen times, and is capitalized thirteen times. In the Oxford it is capitalized only six times. Rotterham capitalizes fourteen times, and other translators still vary the figures. This is an interesting study, and every case may never be positively settled to suit all; hence every one may suit himself. Where it says, "The spirit lusteth against the flesh, and the flesh against the spirit," I would make it refer to the spirit that is in man, and that was "born of the Spirit, and is Spirit." But this antagonism between the two natures in man grows out of the agency of the Holy Spirit. So the difference is not so great, as before stated. Now we have the two natures in the renewed man to distinguish. Much of the difficulty will be overcome when we give the natural good man full credit. We must recognize him not only as intellectual, but moral, social, civil and emotional; loving all that is lovable in natural things. He may be more highly developed morally, socially, etc., than even the spiritual man. He may be more of a philanthropist, more of a patriot, more honest in his dealings. Indeed, he may excel the spiritual man in all things pertaining to nature and natural things. He may be developed into a moralist, with a blameless righteousness as to the law. He may be more benevolent, and in general terms he may be more upright and righteous. The best man outwardly I ever knew was an unconverted man. He was not converted till about fifty years old. I knew him after his conversion, and the difference could not be seen by natural men. The change was more inward than outward. That is, his outward righteousness was not changed, but added to. He was not converted from morality, but from being a moralist. He was taught that he needed more than he had, though he might have had all the righteousness of the law. The law if broken at all, at any time, condemned him. It had no forgiveness for transgressions and no justification for shortcomings. He needed Christ, "the end of law for righteousness to all who believe." Righteous as he was, he was not holy. He did not love God with all his heart, mind, soul and strength. He needed a new nature, which he got when he was born of God. Then he became spiritual in his morality, benevolence, etc. He had always loved me as a friend, but when I met him after his conversion, we met not only as friends, but as brethren in Christ. Joy filled his heart and the tears of joy filled his eyes when we met as brethren in Christ. He was adding to his moral righteousness the righteousness of the Gospel. He had confessed Christ, been baptized, was a member of Christ's body, and was doing all in the name of Christ and for the sake of Christ and through love to Christ. He might have confessed Christ with the mouth, been immersed, joined the church and exercised himself in church duties, as thousands do, without regeneration or change of heart and nature. Yea, he might have done all this without acting the hypocrite. His intentions might have been good, as far as he had been instructed. Yea, his natural emotions may have been stirred at the narration of the death-bed scenes, and the promises made to departed loved ones "to be good and to meet him in heaven." In this way thousands are deceived about their conversion. I beg you, if you are to discern between the natural and spiritual in man; if you would preserve a Regenerated Church Membership, enquire if your candidate for baptism and church membership has been convicted of sin; if he has experienced godly sorrow for sin; if he has experienced contrition of heart and soul; if he has repented; if he has called mightily upon God for mercy; if by faith in Christ as his personal Savior he experiences peace and joy in believing; if he loves the Lord and desires in all things to glorify him; if he loves the children of God and the service of God; search for the evidences of regeneration. The tree must first be good before the fruit can be good. If he wants to be baptized and join the church in order to be saved, tell him that is the broad road that leads to death, and thousands walk together there. If he wants to do these things because he is saved, and as expressions and professions and confessions that he is saved, assure him that "he that does righteousness has been born of God." Not he that does the righteousness that is of the law, and our enquiries don't generally go beyond morality and natural goodness, but search diligently for a righteousness apart from law that pertains to Christ. Christ must not only be his Savior, but his teacher and king. Having been discipled to Christ, he takes Christ for his Lord to rule over him. Ascertain if his obedience grows out of his love to Christ, then show him that his love grows out of regeneration. "Whosoever loves has been begotten of God," and this "love was shed abroad in his heart by the Holy Spirit." See that his obedience is out of a pure heart, a heart purified by faith. Assure him of the order of the spiritual economy of grace. It is not "do and live," for that is the law. The gospel is "live and do." "Created unto good works." Turn his eyes from his own righteousness to salvation by grace, and not of works. Jno. xv. 13, 14 is a good standard to measure by: "Greater love hath no man than this, that a may lay down his life for his friends. Ye are my friends if ye do whatsoever I command you." To know Christ is life everlasting, and if one knows Christ he would lay down his life for him. That is the inward test. Then the outward: "Ye are my friends." Emphasize the "are"—the present tense. In that is the order. It does not read, Ye will become my friends by doing. That is Arminianism—the gospel revised. Make him clear of that deceit through the words ye shall speak unto him. Then emphasize the "I," in contradistinction to Moses or men who make void the commandment of Christ through their tradition. Warn him that the world is full of such commandments of men. "Whosoever" would do "whatsoever" Christ commands is good material for church membership. If he would do these things to be saved he is a natural man, and has not the Spirit. If he would do these things because he is saved, he is a spiritual man. Learn to discern between the natural and the spiritual, or the uncircumcised in heart will destroy the Temple of God, which temple is holy.

I commend the following words of Dr. Austin Phelps:

"What a satire on developed goodness in man is expressed in the tone of the Scriptures towards the best embodiment of the natural virtues! Breathe into nature's good man the most comely of her graces; educate in him the most refined of her sensibilities; develop in him the most magnanimous of her impulses; fashion in him the most docile obedience to her teachings; nurture in him the most elegant and placid of her tastes, so that to the silken judgment of the world his character shall seem to be a paragon of beauty, fair as a star when only one is shining in the sky, yet if that fascinating being—that young man of whom it shall be said that Jesus, beholding him, loved him—have not been changed by the washing of regeneration and renewing of the Holy Chost, the honest eye of God sees him as a naked soul in bondage to the prince of the power of the air."

How much do we need to exercise our senses in

discerning between the natural and the spiritual in man. Not all that seems good in man is good. If "Satan can appear as an angel of light," and his ministers as ministers of righteousness, then how many in our churches may have an outward righteousness only and may be deceiving themselves and others about their salvation? The light must be held up so a man need not be deceived. Many shall say in that day: "Lord, Lord, have we not done so and so in thy name," and many other such Scriptures show something of both the extensive and intensive degree of deception that men practice; yea, honestly practice in this world. The way, the truth, the life, as embodied in Regenerated Church Membership is the only way of escape from the soul-destroying deception of the Natural Goodness in Man.

Chapter X.

In trying to discern between the Natural and Spiritual in the spiritual man, let us look a little at the Motives that prompt service. "The thoughts of the wicked are an abomination unto God," and "the plowing of the wicked is sin;" not that it is wrong to think or wrong to plow, but the motive is wrong. "God is not in all his thoughts"—that is, right thoughts of God; and right thoughts of the right God, as there are gods many and lords many. Many imagine they think of God when it is only an imaginary god. Universalists laud their god of goodness and mercy and power, but he is only a demigod, bereft of holiness and justice. Spiritual thoughts of God are such as ascribe to him perfection in all his attributes. Then his holiness is such that he cannot look upon sin with allowance, and his justice such that he will give a just recompense to every transgression. The "wicked" include moralists, and no such ever had affectionate and worshipful thoughts of the "very" and "only true God." They can't plow like the spiritual man who plows in hope, and plans to glorify God if abundant harvests crown his labor. The other class plan the pulling down of barns and the building of greater that they may store it up for the lust of the flesh. If both plow side by side, there may be no difference outwardly. Indeed, the natural man may excel in plowing and reaping, but the difference in their motives, the moral and spiritual qualities of the act, is like an impassable gulf. The spiritual man can and ought to plow spiritually, thanking God for the strength and facilities and trusting him for the harvest, and promising him a liberal tithing as his expression of thankfulness and dependence. But the natural man is not so, never was, never will be, never can be. That is a height he can't attain for the want of a new heart. So with loving his wife and children. The natural man may even excel in his natural love and devotion to both, because both may be more lovable and he more loving in his nature. But his love stops with the wife and children. If he could recognize God as the giver of both, then his gratitude would be in proportion to benefits received, and he would "praise God all the day long." The spiritual man, for want of such instruction as I am trying to give, may never have exercised himself in loving his wife and children spiritually, but only as a natural man. But he is able to do what the other is not, and he ought so to do. If so, he can glorify God more in loving an inferior wife and children, yea, infinitely more, than the natural man, and in doing so he will have the more joy because his love will be spiritual; that is, a holy recognition of God, from whom comes every good and perfect gift.

The natural man loves only natural things; the spiritual man loves also spiritual things. The two walk and talk together, and you may think there is no difference. Like Sam Jones' two dogs, each has his wagon to guard, but as both families and wagons are traveling together, the dogs may also make a common lot in the journey. You may not know which dog belongs to which wagon, as long as they travel together. But when the wagons part, one going to the right and the other to the left, the dogs quickly show where they belong. So the natural and spiritual man may walk together, both of them moral, intellectual and social, but when the time comes for the roads to part, the difference is seen by each taking the road of his destiny.

The natural man by the restraints of fear and constraints of convictions of selfish interests, may outwardly perform any act of righteousness, but if left unterrified by law, or uninfluenced by love of gain, would act quite differently. He often does what he would not. Also the spiritual man under adverse circumstances and influences may do evil. If so, he does what he would not. If the unregenerate does outward righteousness when he would not, it is no longer he that does it. If the regenerate outwardly does evil, he does what he would not, and it is no longer he that does it. The first does righteousness not from the heart, but from fleshly considerations; hence the reward of his righteousness is in the flesh. And as the other does evil, not from his heart, but from fleshly considerations, his punishment is in the flesh. The reward of neither extends beyond this life.

Having discerned this difference in Motives, let us discern some difference in Emotions. The natural man has good natural emotions, and that is a broad field where Satan sows his tares, "while men sleep." The greatest danger to Regenerated Church Membership comes from this source. Religion, pure and undefiled, is Emotional, and so are all religions, but the emotions are not always pure and undefiled. Indeed, emotion is a prominent characteristic of our holy religion, and because of this Satan has used his wiles and devices in counterfeiting it. We must not, as some have done, discard feeling in religion. Nothing has been more abused and corrupted, and nothing should be more skilfully guarded. Not all whose emotions have been aroused are converted. Let us try to get a right understanding of this important matter.

Man is a sentient being. Whether we approach him through his physical members, mental perceptions, or spiritual motives, the invariable object of our approach or appeal is to produce an impression, a sensation—to move his feelings. With man feeling is life and life is feeling. Whatever cause is adduced; whatever means we use, we hope to effect a change of feeling; then feeling becomes a secondary cause, rebounding from the inner court, affecting the mind and members in turn, as it outwardly works. Paul speaks of those who are "past feeling." Such were "given up" as past recovery. If a man is insensible to your appeal or effort, you can't move him. The body that is insensible to physical appliances, as a galvanic battery, is a dead body. The mind that is unaffected by your argument is dead to you and your object. So of the inner or spiritual man, if unmoved by your moral suasion. Man's five senses, as they are called, are but five avenues to his inner, sentient self. Destroy the optic nerve and you destroy sight. Sight is the sensation made by the object viewed, being impressed on the retina, and this is conveyed through the optic nerve to the inner real man and moves him with emotions, or sensations, pleasurable or unpleasurable, joyous or grievous. So the end and life of sight is feeling. So of the ear. Sounds operate on our feelings, and were so designed, and the ear so constructed. And so of the other senses. Substances are said to throw off their particles imperceptibly small, and these coming in contact with the olfactory nerve, produce sensations, agreeable or disagreeable. But the sensation is called smell. The man who was born blind can not reason correctly about sight, for he has no experimental knowledge of the distinction of colors. He might be able to show that the philosophy of sight is unphilosophical, and to cap the climax he might say that these objects never impressed him with their varying hue. Nevertheless you see, I see, thousands see, and no man's subtle arguments, backed by his own want of experience, can overthrow your faith and experience or mine. Many questions may be asked we cannot answer, but this one thing we know, that whereas he is blind, yet we see. That foundation standeth sure. It being a matter of conscious experience, like toothache, no belief of records or cold logic can destroy it with us. It may keep him from having such experience, but not us. The man who can see and hear but can't smell may reason himself and us out of all philosophies of smell, but so long as we enjoy the fragrance of the rose, or so long as we see the pack of hounds wild and bellowing with excitement over the small particles thrown off by the fox an hour before, we are ready to stand by the fact. The fox passed that way and the hounds know it, because they feel it through the sense of smell, and that feeling is working out and producing those effects. In all these cases and in all others feeling comes in as a witness, and when it has testified, no sort and no amount of counter evidence can overthrow the testimony. But all this by way of illustration.

Coming to the religious life, we see the same primal principles at work. God addresses man as he is, approaches him in his complex nature, with means and motives, and with the mighty power of his Spirit; and the aim and end of all is to change man's feelings—to change his eternity of suffering to an eternity of happiness, and whether arguments to change his mind be used, or motives to change his life, the gracious object of all is to change man's woful experience, and all the exhortations to joy in this life are but the earnests or foretastes of the unspeakable felicities and eternal fruitions contemplated in the divine economy in bringing man to complete happiness with God. Whatever the present duty or trial, the ultimate object of all is our happiness. Why even present afflictions shall work out their counter feelings in a far more exceeding and eternal weight of glory. But this much to emphasize the idea of feeling in a general religious view.

Now trace these principles as they operate in all the steps that grace displayed to save rebellious man. A man in a lost state is said to be blind, in darkness, sick, dead, in bondage to sin, led captive, child of wrath, without hope, at enmity, " heart fully set to do evil," "free from righteousness," "loving sin" and "serving it," etc.

But with the saved man a great change has taken place. A wonderful transition, which must produce a change of feeling, and was so designed. Blind—see; dead—alive; hate—love; love—hate; trouble—peace; mourn—rejoice. Old things gone, ALL things new. God, Christ, Holy Spirit, Word, World, Saints, Sinners, Worship, Songs, prayers, sermons, life, afflictions, persecutions, bereavements, death, grave, resurrection, judgment, eternity—ALL things NEW. The change is not in the record, but in experience.

Revivalists, either through ignorance or ambition, recognizing this important characteristic in religion, have resorted to doubtful means to arouse the emotions of both saints and sinners, and thousands have been deceived about their conversion, and our churches are filled with those whose natural emotions have been revived with deathbed stories, etc., and who have had no spiritual emotions implanted. They want to go to heaven to be with their friends. Watch this deception. Enquire about the changed feelings, about sin and God and his children and Christ and his service. Revival of natural emotions may be good, but new spiritual emotions must be had.

THE FORMAL AND THE SPIRITUAL.

CHAPTER XI.

Having tried to exercise our senses in discerning the Letter and Spirit of the Word, and also the Natural and Spiritual in Man, let us try also to discern the Formal and Spiritual in Religion. The Letter addressed to the Natural man can only lead to Formal Religion. The Spirit which is adapted to the Spiritual man leads to Spiritual Religion. Regenerated Church Membership cannot be maintained unless we discern these differences.

Religion consists of Internals and Externals, both of which need to be watched with jealous care. We will begin with the Internals. The following Scriptures are to be carefully noted at this point: Matt. xiii. 13-16; xxiii. 25-28; Mark iv. 11, 12; Luke viii. 10; John xii. 40; Acts xxviii. 26, 27. I put Hearing as the first of the Internal operations. Whatever of the physical there may be in hearing is of little importance. The mind, soul and spirit are more exercised in hearing than the body. There is a dual hearing. It may be profitable or unprofitable. There is a right kind of hearing and a wrong kind. Hence Christ says: "Take heed how ye hear." Both classes heard him, and the hearing proved either a "savor of death unto death or of life unto life." The right motive must be found here as elsewhere. I preached regularly to an intelligent deacon who was never profited by my preaching. What spiritual members liked, he disliked. He did not like the preacher. He heard from the beginning that he was a doctrinal preacher, and that was enough for him. He heard to find fault. He backslided from the choir to the back seat and then "slid out." The spirit of the hearing was not right. He didn't come to hear what God's word said to him, or if the preacher spoke according to God's word, but he had a standard of his own to try preachers by. There is a great deal of this in our churches, and much of the wrong spirit in hearing is found also among sinners. When they have ears to hear, then they will regard the message as from God to them, and they will hear with a disposition to heed and to hearken and to hasten. They will give attention, and will consider and meditate and ponder. The forgetful hearers of the word will not be profited. Now imagine two saints sitting side by side, and also two sinners. They see the same preacher and hear the same preaching. But different effects are produced; yea, opposite effects. The difference is in the hearing. Not in the physical part, for as far as that is involved there is no difference. The difference is in the internal qualities of the hearing. But putting the best results to the natural hearer, the mind of the natural man may approve the argument and his soul may approve the moral lesson, but the spiritual must be discerned and appropriated, and I think the best lesson to teach the sinner is to teach him his inability to reach the righteous requirement in any duty, and urge him to call upon God for help; and while the calling may be only of the natural man, yet God may have respect unto that, and he may circumcise his ears to hear and his heart to love, and may "open his heart to understand" and " to attend." When saint or sinner tries to hear aright, and asks God for help, he will get that that is lacking, and his hearing will become spiritual, and he will be able to apprehend the things of the Spirit of God.

After hearing comes Conviction, which also may be natural or spiritual. Herod was convicted of all the evil he did, yet he proceeded to shut up John in prison. Under conviction the Pharisees evil entreated the Lord, and his prophets and apostles. Judas was convicted of his wrong and hung himself. "Being convicted in their consciences they went out one by one." The conviction of the natural man tends to exasperation, and may result from reproof and rebuke. This shows the importance of exhortation, that the exasperation may be turned into contrition. I believe here is "the point we know not where, the time we know not when, that turns the destiny of men." We can convict men's minds of sin, but it is the Holy Spirit who convicts the heart and causes godly sorrow that works repentance. And here is seen the necessity of prayer for the Holy Spirit to help in time of need. The Holy Spirit is to be prayed for, and when he comes to our help he will convict the sinner of sin, of righteousness and of condemnation. He alone can turn the natural into spiritual conviction. Be sure the conviction is spiritual or you may defile the temple of God by admitting the uncircumcised in heart. I have had sinners to confess their convictions to me. But what sort were they? They were convinced they ought to do better, to join the church and be baptized and do religion. I have detected many of these cases and kept them back for right convictions. And what are they? Ah! be faithful here. Convince him that he is not only a sinner, but a hell-deserving and hell-bound sinner, and that all the righteousness of his professed reformation would but sink him the deeper in hell, because it would be trampling under foot the blood of the covenant. Convince him that Jesus and Jesus only can deliver him from his just condemnation and can clothe him with the righteousness of God. Then, like the Publican, his conviction will become spiritual, and he will " smite his breast and pray, God be merciful to me a sinner." Then by faith in the sacrifice God has made for sin, he can go down to his house not only forgiven, but justified.

Another Inward exercise springing up in Conviction is Sorrow. But there are two kinds of Sorrow: the worldly sorrow that works death and the godly sorrow that works repentance. Achan was sorry for his sin, and so was Judas, and so are sinners generally when they are caught. It is natural that they should be, nor is it wrong. But they must not stop short of spiritual sorrow, which is "according to God," and "which works repentance not to be regretted."

Then REPENTANCE is also natural and spiritual. It pertains to the mind. Judas repented. Our penitentiaries are full of penitents. Their minds may be fully changed about their sin and its sinfulness, and the deserts of their punishment, and yet they may have an "impenitent heart." Repentance must be "toward God," like David when he cried, "Against thee, thee only, have I sinned, and done this evil in thy sight." It is right for a natural man to repent, and so God commands it of all men everywhere. But the repentance, like the other exercises, must be more than natural, it must be spiritual, and it can't be so until it has respect to God, against whom all sin is committed. Sin not only transgresses the divine law, but it is committed also against God's "goodness and longsuffering and forbearance."

But FAITH may also be natural and not spiritual. Faith may be vain as well as works, and dead as well as works, for the Bible so speaks. Natural men have some sort of faith. Yea, even the devils believe and tremble. The natural man may have faith to work miracles, yea, may do "many wonderful works," and yet it may not be the faith that saves. Simon Magus believed—not believed also, but also believed, and yet he was "in the gall of bitterness and in the bond of iniquity." The natural man may believe that Jesus is the Christ, as well as the devils, and may be orthodox in his faith as to doctrines, and yet be lost. Guard this point. Faith must be EIS Christ. Not only Christ as the Messiah, or Christ as the Savior, but the faith that is spiritual must spring out of a Repentance that is toward God, and that, out of a godly sorrow for sin, and that, out of spiritual conviction that the sinner himself was lost and condemned, yet Christ is the Savior; yea, doth save, yea, hath saved, hath saved him, and that forever. The faith that brings salvation brings peace and joy in lieu of the sorrow and trouble. This is the witness of the Spirit to every true believer.

But LOVE is also natural and spiritual. Sinners love those that love them. Sinners love wife and children and parents and friends, and nature, and morality, and formal religion. Yea, may they not also love and adore God as they see his power, wisdom and goodness displayed in creation and providence? I believe this, and would encourage it, for God must be loved with all the mind and soul, for this great command was given to natural men. Did not the multitudes who followed Christ for the loaves and fishes and for healing, and who spread their garments in his path, crying hozannah—did they not love him? Most surely. And yet the love may not have been spiritual. It may not have been "out of a pure heart fervently." They may have loved his power and goodness and greatness, and this they ought to have done. But did they love his holiness? Did they love him as a Savior from sin? Did they love him because he had saved them from their sins? Here is the test-point, and I beg you preachers to test it, or Regenerated Church Membership may be violated.

There are two kinds of FASTING. Isa. lviii. 3; Joel ii. 13; Matt. vi. 16-18. So also of Mourning. Many widows go sparking in mourning. The widowers are no better, only they have on a broad hat band and not so much outward display. When the outward sign corresponds with the inward feeling, then fasting and mourning are right. If by such means we seek the mercy of God then they are spiritual.

I have referred to these Internals of religion because out of them come the forms. If the Internals are only natural, then the forms are only natural. When the Internals are spiritual, then the forms will be spiritual. With this in mind let us proceed to examine the Externals of religion and discern in them the Formal and the Spiritual.

CHAPTER XII.

"Having a form of godliness, but denying the power thereof: from such turn away." (2 Tim. iii. 5). Dr. Adam Clark says on this: "The original word (morphosis) signifies a draught, a sketch, a summary, and will apply well to those who have all their religion in their creed, confession of faith, catechism, bodies of divinity, etc., while destitute of the life of God in their souls. They also deny that such life or power is here to be experienced or known. They have religion in their creed but none in their hearts. To this summary they add a decent round to their religious observances."

This is Satan's substitute for spiritual religion. Even a regenerated man may become addicted to ritualism, and content himself with the forms, hoping in another world to feel the power. The elect may be deceived in many things, but not in all things. They may be cheated out of much of the allotment of present happiness and usefulness, but not out of salvation of the soul.

But we now proceed to the consideration of Dual Duties in the Externals of Religion.

The forms may be according to the Letter, and yet there may be no power to subdue the will, control the passions, or to transform the life. Even the Externals of Duty are to be spiritually performed, and this is impossible without Regenerated Church Membership. The forms must be according to Letter and Spirit. The natural man can observe forms only in letter, and the Spiritual man may do no better, so he should all the time and with all his heart and by all means seek to be more and more Spiritual, and that in all things. If any man claims to be perfect in this, he deceives himself, and may aim to deceive others, but is not likely to succeed to any alarming extent in the latter.

Let us begin with Confession as the first External in religious duty. This is a duty of the mouth only. A natural man can make any required Confession with the mouth, one about as easy as another, and that is as far as he can go. The Spiritual man may do no more, but he can and ought and would if properly instructed. The mind and emotions may be involved in this physical action, and yet it may not be Spiritual, and can't be unless the heart is first prepared by a purifying faith. When the heart believeth unto righteousness, then the mouth may make confession unto salvation. (Rom. x. 10). A natural man may say with the mouth that Jesus is Lord, for the devils confessed it ; but when the heart says it, it must be by the Holy Spirit. (1 Cor. xii. 3). When Peter, with a loving heart, looked into the face divine and said : "Thou are the Christ, the Son of the living God," Jesus, knowing his heart, said : "Blessed art thou, Simon Bar-jona : for flesh and blood hath not revealed it unto thee, but my Father which is in heaven." (Matt. xvi. 17). The Father not only introduces his Son to us, but reveals him in us ; "and no man knows the Father but the Son, and he to whom the Son will reveal him." (Luke x. 22). When this is done, then the mouth can confess in Spirit and in truth. In this the true sense : "Whosoever shall confess that Jesus is the

Son of God, God dwelleth in him, and he in God." (1 John iv. 15). All who rightly confess Christ before men, he will confess before the Father and before the angels; but the confession must be Spiritual and not with the mouth only.

So Baptism may have the form according to the letter, and that only, and, if so, it has not the power. If John the Baptist had baptized the multitudes who applied for baptism (see Matt. iii. 7–10 and Luke iii. 7–9), it would perhaps have sealed their damnation. Why? Because they were destitute of the Spiritual prerequisites to baptism, and hence their baptism could only have been in form according to the letter.

A man must first believe in Christ, and "whosoever believeth in the Son of God hath the witness in himself" (1 John v. 10); "hath everlasting life, and shall not come into condemnation" (John v. 24); "has been born of God" (1 John v. 1) and "overcometh the world" (1 John v. 4–5), "is justified" (Rom. v. 1). Yea, he must have the blessings predicated of Repentance, Faith, Love, Confession, or baptism will lead him away and astray, and that to his own destruction. How can a man obey in Spirit without Spritual qualification? If Spiritual fitness is not inquired into, then soon it will not be required. You need not expect it if you don't exact it; if not taught it will not be sought; if not held it will not be had. If a candidate goes down into the water without having died to sin—and that means freedom from sin—

and with no newness of life, then his baptism, so called, would be a solemn profession of falsehood. Rom. vi. 1--11 has no reference to baptism of the Holy Spirit, or by the Holy Spirit, or in the Holy Spirit, yet it is Spiritual baptism. It is not the natural man conforming to the letter, but the Spiritual man conforming to both Letter and Spirit of baptism. "How shall we who died to sin, live any longer therein? Or, are you ignorant, that all we who were baptized unto Jesus Christ, were baptized unto his death? We were buried, therefore, with him through baptism unto death; that as Christ was raised from the dead through the glory of the Father, so we also should walk in newness of life. For if we have become united with the likeness of his death, we shall be with that of his resurrection also. Knowing this, that our old man was crucified with him, that the body of sin might be destroyed, in order that we might no more be in bondage to sin. And if we died with Christ, we believe that we shall also live with him; knowing that Christ being raised from the dead, dies no more; death has no more dominion over him. For the death that he died, he died to sin once for all; but the life that he lives, he lives to God. Thus reckon ye also yourselves to be dead to sin but alive to God in Christ Jesus."

How inconceivably high does this lift us above the idea of a natural man submitting to a sacrament in order to be saved. How degrading the thought to a spiritual man. I would prefer idolatry in any of its forms to such a perversion of a holy ordinance and its implied holy doctrines. No likeness of any god can save any man from anything, not even any likeness of the true God or his Christ. We were saved by the death and resurrection of Christ, and not by the likeness of it. There is no more salvation in baptism than any other likeness of things or beings. If looking through the images to the gods is idolatry, so looking through this likeness to the reality is idolatry also. We are not allowed to have any likeness of God or of Christ, but baptism, a likeness of salvation, is allowed and ordained as the profession of our hope before men. It is a figure of our salvation, not the putting away the filth of the flesh which is sin, but the answer of a good conscience by the resurrection of Christ. How was the answering conscience made good? "How much more shall the blood of Christ . . . purge your conscience from dead works to serve the living God." (Heb. ix. 14). "And the worshippers once purged should have no more conscience of sins." (Heb. x. 2). " Let us draw near with a true heart in full assurance of faith, having our hearts sprinkled from an evil conscience and our bodies washed with pure water. Let us hold fast the profession of our hope without wavering; for he is faithful that promised." (Heb. x. 22-24). Baptists are indeed distinguished for keeping the blood before water and Christ before the church. If baptism is the putting on of Christ and identifies us as Christians, ought we not to be Christians before we put on Christ? If the baptism of infants is infant baptism, and the baptism of believers is believers' baptism, then is not the baptism of Christians Christian baptism? And if so, where can you find Christian baptism except among the Baptists? Certainly no others hold it as the rule.

Also the Lord's Supper must be observed spiritually as well as in letter. The one body, the one loaf, the one cup and the tarrying one for another so as to eat and drink together, constitute the letter and the form, but all this may be observed not discerning the Lord's body and blood in the emblems, and not discerning our interest in the sacrifice by the appropriating act of eating and drinking. And what interest have we? A common interest. A common interest with whom? With each other and with Christ. Hence it is called communion of the body and blood of Christ. That means fellowship or partnership with each other and with Christ in the benefits of his death and resurrection. From a failure to discern this many in the church at Corinth (and in every other church) "are weak and sickly and many sleep." The form, the right form, must be spiritualized or there will be no power. The unleavened bread and the wine that has purged itself of impurities bespeak the sinlessness of the victim sacrificed. The church partaking of them declares that it too is to be sharer in his holiness—" a glorious church, not having spot or wrinkle or any such thing." Where there are divisions and schisms the Lord's Supper can't be eaten except in form, for the spiritual lesson of unity is destroyed, as only an undivided body can eat it. (1 Cor. xi. 18, 20). Individual cups and a plate of crackers destroys the Spiritual lesson of unity of the body. The Spirit can't be right unless the form is right. This is as true of the Supper as it is of baptism.

So Giving may be right in form and letter and wrong in Spirit. Wrong giving is referred to in Matt. vi. 1-4; Acts v. 1-10 and viii. 18-20, etc., and right giving is referred to in Matt. x. 8; Mark ix. 41; Rom. viii. 8; 2 Cor. ix. 7, etc. Follow out these and other references and teach the people how to give so as to be blessed, and they will soon learn not only to give freely, but liberally and always "as unto the Lord."

So you must teach about Singing. This may be in exact accord with the letter and understanding and not in the Spirit. (Eph. v. 19 and Col. iii. 16, etc.) There is a great deal of melody in the mouth when singing to men, and no melody in the heart singing unto the Lord. Without the latter it is all harmonic foolishness and fuss, so far as praise is concerned. It may be good for a social, but it is bad for worship, because they don't sing unto the Lord. If we pray unto the Lord why not sing unto him? The same importance must be attached to Praying. (Matt. i. 5-15). Much praying is to men, to be seen or heard of men, and though the forms may be impressive, and the words elegant and eloquent, it is all abomination unto the Lord. We may call on God with the lips while the heart is far from him. We must learn to "lift up holy hands without wrath and doubting," and "call on the Lord out of a pure heart." In prayer we have much of the form and little of the power.

The same is true of Preaching. Phil. i. 15-17 and 2 Cor. xi. 13-15 are examples of bad preaching. Preachers must test and prove themselves in their high calling lest they preach to please men and to be rewarded of men rather than study to show themselves approved unto God.

Discipline may be according to the literal instructions given in Matt. xviii., and yet it may not be done "to gain a brother," but to make gain of him, or to destroy him. A striking example of form and letter without Spirit is seen in Judas kissing the Lord. It was the kiss of death because it was in letter and not in Spirit. A striking example of form and power is seen in the woman who touches the hem of his garment. It was the touch of faith and love, and both she and Christ felt the power of it. The one touch of finger to hem had more power than Judas's many touches of lip to lip. One was the savor of life, the other of death. The letter (only) killeth. The Spirit (with the letter) gives life.

REGENERATED CHURCH MEMBERSHIP.

CHAPTER XIII.

The greatest danger to Regenerated Church Membership grows out of a failure to distinguish between morality and spirituality. We have tried to make clear this distinction apart from church membership. The question now to be considered is, was it this spiritual kind of material that in the beginning was put into the church—God's spiritual temple? There is an exception, but I think it helps to establish the rule. Christ knew from the beginning that Judas was a devil, yet he chose him, and put upon him all the honors that belong to a true disciple. He preached, wrought miracles, was treasurer, and had the best associations and influences that were ever provided for men. He was solemnly warned at the last supper, and was driven out on his devilish mission; and in the face of all this, he sold his Master and betrayed him with a kiss. All this was necessary according to the divine purpose and plan, and as none but a devil could do a devil's work, a devil was chosen to do it. Now if Judas, an unconverted man in the church, with all of his favorable advantages, was not deterred by detection and exposure "before the act" from its commission, on what ground can we found a hope that the church is the institution for a sinner to join? Yet the Catholic and Protestant world hold to this idea, and the writer entertains grave apprehension that we Baptists, in a large measure, have imbibed the damnable heresy. I fear many of our evangelists think that joining the church might do the sinner good, and with this salve on their doubting consciences they proceed to add fame to their name by large additions as a seal to their ministry.

But how was it in the beginning? With Judas out, the purged church was found tarrying in Jerusalem in protracted prayer meeting waiting for the promised enduement of power from on high. (Acts i). In the second chapter we find they all continued with one accord in one place. Not an unconverted person among them. They were all filled with the Holy Spirit, and spake as the Spirit gave them utterance. Their preaching was greatly blessed, and many were convicted of sin, and when they cried out asking what they must do, they were not told to join the church for salvation. They were told to repent and be baptized, trusting in the name of Jesus Christ for the remission of sins, and they (as well as the others) should receive the gift of the Holy Spirit. Peter preached the same gospel in Acts ii. 38 that he preached in Acts x. 43. The Greek idiom requires the above rendering. In the Nashville Debate Elder J. A. Harding says on page 465 " that the man to whom Jesus gave the keys of the kingdom of heaven told convicted sinners to repent and be baptized, trusting in Jesus for the remission of sins, and he should receive the gift of the Holy Ghost." On page 560 he says: "And in answer to their cry he told them to repent, and be baptized, trusting in the name of Jesus for the remission of their sins." Similar language is found on pp. 57, 58, 438, 486, 497, 500 and 518. David Lipscomb has also professed conversion to the same view. But this will come up again.

The change from the painful conviction of sin to the glad reception of the Word is evidence. To be publicly baptized in the name of Jesus Christ whom they had crucified, and with wicked hands had slain, and that in the face of fiery persecution, is evidence again; and if further evidence is wanted it is abundantly supplied in what follows:

"And they continued steadfastly in the apostles' doctrine and fellowship, and in breaking of bread, and in prayers. And all that believed were together, and had all things common; And sold their possessions and goods, and parted them to all, as every man had need. And they, continuing daily with one accord in the temple, and breaking bread from house to house, did eat their meat with gladness and singleness of heart, Praising God, and having favor with all the people. And the Lord added to the church daily such as should be saved."

The last words, if rightly translated, render this doctrine doubtful. Did the Lord add to the church the saved or such as should be saved? If such as should be saved, the Catholics and Protestants are right and the Baptists wrong. If they were saved before they were added, the Baptists are right and the others wrong. The Catholic Bible reads: "And the Lord added daily to their society such as should be saved." King James follows with the "such as should be saved." This makes the salvation prospective, and as all men should be saved, then all should join the church, even infants.

To keep one out of the church until he is saved, and saved forever, is peculiarly Baptist doctrine, and we claim that the text rightly translated will prove it. I will introduce a few translations here, just such as have come to hand; also a few commentaries. Were they saved before added or added before saved? That is the question of questions, and upon it rests the doctrine of Regenerated Church Membership.

The Bible Union has it: "And the Lord added to the church daily those who are saved." Broadus, Hovey and Weston have it: "And the Lord added together daily those who were being saved." The Oxford Revision has it: "Those that were being saved." The American Committee in appendix recommends, "Those that were saved" for "those that were being saved." Frequent reference is made by commentators to 1 Cor. i. 18 and 2 Cor. ii. 15, where King James has it, "are saved." Murdock's Translation of the Syriac has it: "The Lord added daily to the assembly those who became alive."

He translates life instead of salvation uniformly. Englishman's Concordance says: "Literally the saved." (See Sozo, p. 612). Doddridge has it: "Those happy souls who were saved." Sawyer says: "The Lord added the saved day by day to the assembly (church)." Jamison, Faucett and Brown say: "Kept adding to the church daily the saved." Samuel Williams: "Those that were saved." Alexander Campbell in Living Oracles has it: "The Lord added daily the saved to the congregation." In Campbell-Rice Debate, page 436, he quotes the passage in the same words. On page 459 he has church in the place of assembly. H. T. Anderson (Campbellite) has it: "The Lord added the saved daily to the church." Rotherham (Campbellite) says: "The Lord was adding those being saved day by day together." Emphatic Diaglott: "The Lord daily added those being saved to the congregation." McGarvey (Campbellite) translates: "And the Lord added those saved every day to the church." In a note on page 50 he adds: "Those added to the church were not such as should be saved, but the saved. . . . Luke speaks not of those who daily embrace the means of salvation, but of those who were saved. . . . It is not an inception of the saving work of which Luke speaks, but the salvation referred to is complete, the parties spoken of being called the saved. . . . That men should join the church, not as a means of obtaining pardon, but because they have already obtained it."

Considering the source, this is wonderful testimony. We will have occasion to refer to it again in order to give the writer's peculiar application. Jacobus says: "Rather the saved, or those who were saved. 1 Cor. i. 18 and 2 Cor. ii. 15." Comprehensive Commentary says in note: "The saved, or placed in a state of salvation." Lyman Abbott says: "Only those were accepted in the church who themselves professed to accept salvation through Jesus Christ as their Savior. Conversion was a condition of church membership." Homiletical Commentary has it thus: "A PROSPEROUS CHURCH. First, increasing in numbers. Second, increasing in numbers daily. Third, increasing through the addition of saved souls. Fourth, by additions made by the Lord. The qualification for church membership was conversion at the outset. The church was to be made up of regenerate souls. The apostles filled with the Holy Spirit set as conditions of membership true conversion and a public confession of a sound faith." Adam Clark says, "Were saved from their sins," and adds: "The church of Christ was made up of saints. Sinners were not permitted to incorporate themselves with it. Our translation 'should be saved' is improper and insupportable. The original means simply and solely those then saved." This is strong testimony from an unexpected source, as Methodists boldly denounce the doctrine of Regenerated Church Membership, and claim that joining the church and baptism and the Lord's Supper are sacraments and means of grace to be used in the salvation of sinners. This they have done in the face of Adam Clark's and also Wesley's translation, which reads: "And the Lord added daily to the church those who were saved." This clearly puts salvation before the church.

Thayer says of the word translated saved that it is opposed to apollumi—perish; and under that word he says: "It must be borne in mind that ... eternal life begins on earth just as soon as one becomes united to Christ by faith. Rom. ii. 12; 1 Cor. viii. 11; xv. 18; 2 Pet. iii. 9. Hence hoi soozomenoi, they to whom it belongs to partake of salvation, and hoi apollumenoi, those to whom it belongs to perish, or to be consigned to eternal misery, are contrasted by Paul. 1 Cor. i. 18; 2 Cor. ii. 15; iv. 3; 2 Thess. ii. 10." See also Luke ix. 24, 56; Jno. iii. 15, 16; v. 24; vi. 40; x. 28; Rom. v. 9, 10; Heb. x. 39 and many such, which show that the salvation professed at faith is not simply as Wesley and Clark try to modify, a salvation from past sins only, but salvation from hell, from wrath to come, complete and eternal salvation. Candidates for baptism ought to be taught that they cannot perish, but that they have everlasting life, and cannot come into condemnation; so that they can truly profess in baptism that if they have been planted together in the likeness of his death they will be also in his resurrection.

Who but Baptists can boast so much of God's

grace through faith before baptism and the church? Who is so free as we from baptismal regeneration and church salvation? Do not those who believe in these heresies acknowledge our doctrine of Regenerated Church Membership when they resort to the infantile rite for "regeneration and engrafting into the body of Christ?" McGarvey thinks they are saved before joining the church because baptized before joining the church; and when he wrote his Commentary he believed there was no salvation without immersion. Of course he is opposed by all his brethren and sisters and their children in putting salvation before the church, for they all say baptized into Christ, that is, Christ's body, or the church, and if baptized into it, they can't be saved before either baptism or the church. So Mr. Harding, in being baptized, trusting in the name of Jesus Christ for the remission of sins, means trusting Jesus Christ to remit their sins in baptism, and that really means trusting baptism for the remission of sins, as no one from his standpoint can trust Christ for remission apart from baptism, which makes Christ depend on the believer's baptism.

But Baptists believe that we are saved before the church and baptism too; for faith is a prerequisite to baptism, and salvation and remission and justification and other blessings of salvation are predicated of faith.

Acts ii. 47 undoubtedly puts salvation before the church. But this is not the only Scripture that just-

92   DISTINGUISHING DOCTRINES

ifies this Distinguishing Doctrine of Baptists. So with another short lesson we must consider other Scriptures and arguments on this subject of momentous importance. Then we will begin to consider what is implied in church membership.

Chapter XIV.

Before considering other Scriptures on this subject, let us note two passages that have been united to offset Acts ii. 47. Errorrists seem never to weary in hunting for exceptions in order to neutralize the general rule. They think they have this in Acts. xi. 24 and v. 14, which put together read: "And much people was added to the Lord." "And believers were the more added to the Lord, multitudes both of men and women." The questions asked are: What sort of people were added to the Lord? Answer believers. Then how are believers added to the Lord? They answer by baptism. The claim is, that believers as such are not added to the Lord, and something besides faith is necessary, hence baptism is necessary to add believers to the Lord.

I answer first, that the Scriptures nowhere say that baptism adds believers to the Lord, unless it is in the expression baptized eis Christ, eis his name. But believe eis Christ and eis his name occur much oftener, and if eis in one case suggests the uniting act, it must also in the other. Nor does the context of either passage intimate that baptism was administered, but is rather against it. Rottherham's translation which claims to be literal renders Acts v. 14: "Nevertheless, the more were being added, such as were believing in the Lord." The margin of the Ox. Rev. here supports this. So that settles this passage in line with all the scriptures on the subject. The Epistles addressed to the churches recognize them, not as seekers or probationers, but as saved persons. Rom. i. 7. "To all that be in Rome, beloved of God, called saints." Not "called to be saints," as King James has it. "To be" is not in the original. These words were also supplied in 1 Cor. i. 2, and no doubt would have been in all other places if it could have been done. If the Lord added to the church such as should be saved, then of course they were called to be saints. But if they were saved before they were added, then they were saints before they were added. Hence they were called saints, that is, holy ones. Saint is the characteristic name of God's people both in the Old and New Scriptures. Enoch, the seventh from Adam, foresaw the Lord coming with ten thousand of his saints. David said "Precious in the sight of the Lord is the death of his saints." Daniel said the saints of the most high shall take the kingdom and possess the kingdom forever, even forever and forever, For 1,260 years Rome was drunk on the blood of the saints. And after the Millennium Satan and his hosts will compass the camp of the saints about, and then the final separation of saints and sinners will occur and the final and eternal verdict will be: He that is a sinner let him be a sinner still and he that is a saint (holy) let him be a saint still. The name Christian is of the earth earthy, because sectarian; the name saint is from heaven. It will very much strenghten your faith in this doctrine if you will carefully read the opening addresses. viz.: Rom. i. 6-8 ; 1 Cor. i. 1-9; 2 Cor. i. 1-2; Gal. i. 1-5; Eph. i. 1-2; Phil. i. 1-6; Col. i. 1-6; 1 Thes. i. 1-10; 2 Thes. i. 1-5. See also the addresses of Peter and Jude, and those in Revelation to the Seven Churches of Asia. Neither in these opening addresses, nor any where in those letters is there a class in the churches recognized as seekers or probationers. See especially Rom. v. 1, 2, 11. 1 Cor. iii. 9-17; Gal. iii 1-4; v. 1; Eph. i. 13; ii. 1-22; 1 P. ii. 1-5; and 2 Thes. ii. 13.

But it may be asked if Baptists do not take the unregenerate into their churches? Undoubtedly they do. Then it is asked, what is the difference? I answer, much every way. Others do it knowingly and intentionally, and Baptists are supposed to do it ignorantly and unintentionally, and in this difference is the moral quality of the acts. The difference is the same as the killing of a man intentionally and unintentionally. Indeed, in this matter of receiving the unconverted into the church, the difference may be greater, as more is involved. The life of the soul is greater than that of the body. But may not the difference be widened in another item? Baptists teach that it is wrong to take sinners into the church, and they teach the sinner it is the wrong place for him, and they require the sinner to profess a change of heart or they will not receive him. Sinners often deceive themselves and the preacher and the church, and thus get in "privily" and "unawares" as they did in Apostolic days. Then like Paul we "would they were cut off." Others say it is right to take them in and keep them in. Now if a man or body of men (as Anarchists) say it is right to kill, and follow that as a profession, then their intentional killing is worse than in the first supposed case, as they justify their sin. So those who teach this error and follow it as a profession are more guilty than a Baptist would be if he should in a single case knowingly take in the unconverted. If a Baptist preacher should do such a thing, and avow it as his doctrine, he would be deposed from the ministry if not excluded from the church; and if not, the church would be excluded from any Baptist Association of churches. It is an error that cannot be tolerated because it defiles and destroys the Temple of God, which temple is holy. At the judgment day the son of man will send forth his angels and they shall gather out of his kingdom all things that offend and them that do iniquity, and shall cast them into a furnace of fire; there shall be weeping and wailing and gnashing of teeth. Then shall the righteous—the good seed— the children of the kingdom, shine forth as the sun in the kingdom of their father. Matt. xiii. 36-43. Again, the kingdom of heaven is like a net cast into the sea, and gathered together of every kind, which, when it was full, they drew upon the beach, and sat down and gathered the good into vessels, but cast the bad away. So will it be in the end of the age. The angels will go forth and will separate the wicked from the midst of the righteous, and will cast them into the furnace of fire; there will be the weeping and the gnashing of teeth (Matt. xiii. 47-50). The children of the "wicked one" got in by the agency of the devil, and the bad fish were not intentionally caught.

Do you reply that the field is the world. Be it so. But the kingdom of heaven is like that, with emphasis on the latter part—the separation of the righteous and wicked. If there is no fellowship between the righteous and the wicked and the "unbeliever has no portion with the believer" (2 Cor. vi. 14-18); and as the intermarriage of such is forbidden by the words: "Only in the Lord" (1 Cor. vii. 39); and as they are separated in the intermediate state by an impassable gulf (Luke xvi. 36); and as at last the wicked are to be cast into hell; and as the Scriptures enjoin the exclusion of the unconverted from the church, then woe to the man who in the face of all this will bring them into the church. Did the tares by association in the field become wheat? Did the bad fish by association in the net become good? Did Judas by association with Jesus and the Apostles and holy women become good? Does association in marriage or in the family produce conversion? NEVER. If it is from association Christ would have ordained association for the conversion of the world. The wife may save the husband or the husband the wife (1 Cor. vii. 16), etc., but never by association, but by more powerful means than that. And yet blind guides are zealous to get sinners into the church to be saved by association. Oh! ministers of Christ, old and young! Here is the temptation and the crying sin of the age. Ambition to be counted successful in revivals, and to add so many to the church in a year, may lead you to make this merchandise of souls. Crucify, Crucify, this unholy ambition. Put it to death and have it buried in the sea of God's forgetfulness, lest these deceived souls rise up in the judgment and condemn you. What God has joined together let not man put asunder—and vice versa.

As intimated above, the Exclusion of the Unworthy from the church is another argument in favor of Regenerated Church Membership. 1. A man who will not conform to the law of love and fellowship is to be excluded (Matt. xviii. 15-18). Christ's disciples were to be known by the love they had one for another (John xiii. 34-35 and xv. 13). Love is the fulfilling of the law, and the law forbids the sinning both against God and one another, and the man who cannot be reconciled to his brother is not fit for the kingdom of heaven, nor for the church of the living God. Those that cause divisions and offenses contrary to the doctrine once for all delivered, are not to be taken in or kept in, but avoided. "For they that are such serve not our Lord Jesus Christ, but this own ambition; and by good words and fair speeches deceived the hearts of the simple" (Rom. xvi. 17-18). In 1 Cor. v. we learn that the immoral man in the church leavened the whole lump, and the church was exhorted to purge out the leaven that they might be a new lump, as they were unleavened. They must not eat or keep company with any bad character, not in the world, for then they must needs get out of the world; but if any one called a brother be a fornicator or drunkard or extortioner, etc., he was to be put away from their church fellowship. So also 2 Thes. iii. 6: "Now we charge you brethren in the name of our Lord Jesus Christ, that ye withdraw yourselves from every brother that walketh disorderly, and not after the tradition which ye received of us." Also verse 16: "If any man obey not our word by this epistle, note that man, and have no company with him, that he may be ashamed."

If the ungodly should be turned out of the church, why take them in? I believe that nearly all our church troubles come from the unconverted. It is a rare case that one noted for piety will divide a church, unless it ought to be divided. I never knew a man or woman in the church, noted for piety and prayer and good works, that tried to lower the standard of morals or doctrine of the church to that demanded by the world. I have known many churches to split on this very issue, and I believe that nine-tenths of our churches ought to split, and that right away; and if so, I believe the regenerated would gravitate together and to the truth, and that the unregenerated, whether in the minority or majority, would like-wise flock together, and that with a zeal that is not according to knowledge and with a spirit that is not of God. If the churches can't exclude the unregenerate, let them split, so the churches again can become the light of the world and the salt of the earth.

I will close this first division of my subject embraced in the term Regeneration with a brief answer to a difficult question and then we will take up Church Membership. The question proposed may be stated thus: Since "the natural man cannot discern spiritual things," and since "they that are in the flesh cannot please God," ought natural men in any way try to love and serve God, and ought we to encourage them in it. Last year the Christian Herald had a lengthy symposium on Receiving contributions from Saloonists. This is but a specific and extreme case under the general rule of receiving contributions from sinners; and contribution is but one item under the general rule of encouraging sinners to do good.

I think all men should be encouraged and exhorted to do good in all practical and lawful ways. True, they can do nothing perfectly, but who can? Even the spiritual man don't do all things spiritually. If the spiritual man gives as a natural man, that is from the force of circumstances and not cheerfully and liberally and for the glory of God, then what better is his gift? Indeed, if the unconverted man gives the best he can according to his natural ability, and the converted does not give the best he can according to his spiritual ability, and God will judge each according to his ability to perform, then is not the difference in favor of the sinner? Again; if about half of our membership is unconverted, who can draw the line that will make it right for one side to give and wrong for the other? Christ never condemned the unconverted Jews for giving, but showed them the defect in the motive of their giving—"to be seen of men." So, of praying and fasting. The Ninevites fasted and prayed and repented and confessed, and God heard them and saved them from the impending curse. Ungodly men ought to give thanks, and sing praises to God, the best they can. The law is for the ungodly and that says they must do right and must not do wrong, and the law covers the whole ground. Sinners ought to read God's word, hear, consider, search, seek, heed, hearken, repent, believe, obey.

There was a rich young ruler who said he had kept the law from his youth up, and when Jesus heard that, "he loved him" and told him what he lacked to be saved. When Jesus and Peter were told that the Centurion was worthy, for he had built for them a Synagogue, did not the liberality commend them in both cases? Did not God encourage the natural Jews to worship and serve him in all appointed ways? And yet Paul said: "My hearts' desire and prayer to God for Israel is that they might be saved."

When Christ went into Jerusalem riding upon an ass' colt, the multitudes spread their garments in the way, and those that went before, and those that went behind, cried: "Hosanna to the Son of David. Blessed is he that cometh in the name of the Lord. Hosanna in the highest." "And Jesus went into the temple and cast out those who had turned the house of prayer into a den of thieves. And the blind and the lame came into the temple and were healed. And when the chief priests and scribes saw the wonderful things that he did, and the children crying in the temple, saying Hosanna to the Son of David, they were sore displeased and said unto him, Hearest thou what these say? And Jesus saith unto them, Yea; have you never read, out of the mouth of babes and sucklings, thou hast perfected praise (Matt. xxi. 7-16)?" In Rom. ii. 20, Paul said the Jews were teachers of babes, and Timothy from infancy was taught the Holy Scriptures. So these babes and sucklings had learned the song from the multitudes as Christ came in, and they followed him in the temple singing the same song, and Christ called it the perfection of praise. Or as David has it: "Out of the mouth of babes and sucklings hast thou ordained strength, because of thine enemies, that thou mightest still the enemy and the avenger" (Ps. viii. 2). Here is a wonderful lesson, but my limits are reached, and I must close by saying, there are two things from which sinners are barred, viz., from joining the church, and from the holy ordinances. Not from the meetings of the church (1 Cor. xiv. 23), but from membership in the church, as the church was designed as a company of the saved; and from its ordinances which are spiritual declarations and professions. I know no other restrictions laid upon the unregenerate. Church prerogatives such as voting, officers, and ordinances must necessarily be restricted. But singing and praying and giving, etc., are not church prerogatives, but are as old as the race, and the prerogatives of all.

Last thought. Blessed be God, the knowledge I have tried to impart on this subject is not necessary to salvation, nor is a knowledge of the philosophy of nutrition necessary to the proper eating of food; yet, knowledge is profitable in all good things, and my prayer is that we may all be filled with the full knowledge of his will in all spiritual wisdom and understanding (Col. i. 9).

Chapter XV.

It is not enough that one be regenerated and saved; he should be added to the church. Not only united to Christ for salvation, but also united to one another for service. In union there is strength. If one can chase a thousand and two put ten thousand to flight, then the combined effort of two increases the strength tenfold. Two horses pulling together may not pull ten times as much as one, but in spiritual things I don't believe the Scripture is an exaggeration. Christ sent them two and two to teach them the value of combined effort. I believe a church of two or three, meeting with one accord in one place, with one mind, one heart and one purpose, striving together for the faith of the gospel, can accomplish more than a church of a thousand members in discord. I believe the words of Christ in Matt. xviii. 19 are true. I would render them thus: "Again I say unto you, that if two of you shall agree on earth, as touching any business you crave to accomplish, it shall be done for them of my Father who is in heaven." "For where two or three are gathered together in my name, there am I in the midst of them." The context compels the conclusion that Christ was speaking of church work Wherever two or three persons live together, they should talk together and pray together and work together and labor together for the spread of the Kingdom and the upbuilding of the church. The number in the church should be increased as far as practicable and no further. If a multitude of believers should disturb the union and defeat the co-operation, then the multitude should be divided and the church multiplied. This is exactly what was done in Jerusalem. Let the called out be called together for the work of the Lord. Let the number be bound together and to the Lord by faith and hope and love, and let the union be such as Christ prayed for in the seventeenth chapter of John, and such as Paul described in 1 Cor. i. 9-13, and you have a concept of a paragon picture of a church and church membership. As a man's family obligations are confined to the family of which he is a member, so his church obligations are confined to the church of which he is a member. And as a man's family obligations would be destroyed by extending the family to the whole race, so church obligations would be destroyed by extending the church to all the saved. A man's affection for his "one wife" is a thousand times stronger than his affection for all women. A man's affections and obligations are not susceptible of infinite divisions. They may be extended to the family and to the church, but there are limitations, which in most cases are soon reached. The divine philosophy is seen in this Scripture: "If a man loves not his brother whom he has seen, how can he love God whom he hath not seen?." The emphasis is on the seeing, for in that is the knowing. From this we make another statement as true: If a man loves not his brother whom he has seen, how can he love a brother whom he has not seen? When a man boasts that he loves all the children of God everywhere alike, he is simply talking gush and nonsense. The best of men have only a measure of love, and, like a measure of water, if spread too wide, it will be too shallow. The destruction is in the spreading. As a man can destroy his church obligation by enlaging the church, so can he destroy his family affection and obligation by an imaginary spreading of the family. Christ who made man knew what was in him, and hence gave a church constitution and rules adapted to his limited capacities, and to the church's upbuilding. These prefatory remarks lead us into the investigation of the Constitution and Polity of the church Christ built, and as this was designed to be unchanged and unchangeable, the Perpetuity of the church should claim a part of our attention. Qualifications for membership and principles of government in all institutions of men are considered of great importance.

Since the foundation of the world nothing has been so misunderstood and misrepresented as the church question. Providence has thrust the question to the front and a thorough investigation is demanded. Let us rehearse the matter from the beginning and expound it in order as far as we go. Let us first take the testimony of Christ and then of the apostles. The first use of the word is in Matt. xvi. 18: "On this rock I will build my church, and the gates of Hades shall not prevail against it."

In this expression of Christ's thought he intended to give us concerning the church the conception of his mind and the embodiment of his authority on the earth to the end of time. What did he build? How did he build it? Was the construction such as to prevent destruction?. These questions properly answered will give us a perception of the divine conception.

First, his church was (is), as we have tried to show, a building designed to be composed of regenerated persons. In the second chapter of Ephesians we have a description of those who were " dead in trespasses and sins," " saved by grace through faith," "Jews and Gentiles," "reconciled in one body," "fellow-citizens of the saints, and of the household of God," built upon the foundation of the apostles and prophets, Jesus Christ being the chief cornerstone, in whom every building fitly framed together groweth unto a holy temple in the Lord; in whom ye also are builded together for a habitation of God through the Spirit." This language was addressed to "saints and to the faithful in Christ Jesus" which were at Ephesus, and to them certainly as a church, as the Scripture above implies. If this needs further confirmation read chapter iv. 2-5: "With all lowliness and meekness, with long suffering, forbearing one another in love; endeavoring to keep the unity of the Spirit in the bonds of peace. One body, one Spirit, even as ye are called in one hope of your calling; one Lord, one faith, one baptism," etc. These words imply both relationship and organization. See also verse 16: "From whom the whole body fitly framed together and compacted," etc. This church at Ephesus was a building, and we now look to 2 Peter ii. 2–5 for a further description of the material: "As newborn babes, desire the sincere milk of the word that ye may grow thereby; if so be ye have tasted that the Lord is gracious. . . . Ye also as living stones are built up a spiritual house, a holy priesthood, to offer up spiritual sacrifices acceptable to God by Jesus Christ." This is Peter's description of a church of Christ. Now, add Paul's words in 1 Cor. iii. 9, 16, 17: "For we are laborers together with God; ye are God's husbandry, God's building. . . . Know ye not that ye are the temple of God, and that the Spirit of God dwelleth in you? If any man defile the temple of God, him will God destroy." Here the church of Corinth is called God's field, with living, growing, fruit-bearing plants; or God's building, composed of Peter's living stones, and this building was compacted together and the members were laborers together with God. To such a building or church the Lord in the beginning added daily the saved. This is what Christ built as his church. He built it for the glory of his Father, and "unto him" there was to be "glory in the church by Christ Jesus throughout all generations of the ages." Eph. iii. 21. So the gates of hades have not prevailed against it. Notice, Christ built but one church. If that was a universal church, composed of all the saved in all ages, infants and idiots included, then the congregational church was not the divine conception, and is not divine unless he built two churches. Baptists agree that it was one of the two. All other terms used to express territorial or denominational conceptions of the church are unscriptural and need not be noticed. Which was the divine conception in the text, the congregational or universal church? This is our first question, and there are several lines of investigation that seem to compel one answer. Christ certainly agrees with himself, and as he is "the true and faithful witness," we will consider his testimony on the meaning of the word church in his first use of it.

Matt. xviii. 17, 18 gives the conception of Christ's mind and the embodiment of his authority on the earth, in his second use of the term church, "If he neglect to hear them tell it to the church, but if he neglect to hear the church, let him be unto thee as a heathen man and a publican. Verily I say unto you, whatsoever ye shall bind on earth shall be bound in heaven, and whatsoever ye shall loose on earth shall be loosed in heaven." In this passage Baptists have no difficulty or disagreement as to what the church is. It was not a univeral, catholic, national, provincial, sectional or denominational church. Nor was it a part of a church, as a ruling officer or a presbytery, for we are agreed that congregationalism not only limits authority to the congregation, but extends authority to all in the congregation. On this, the second use of the word, Christ certainly had the congregational conception, for grievances cannot be told to any other kind of a church, and parts of a church, as a so-called ruling officer and presbytery are never conceived of as a church. So the testimony of the Lord here is right and simple and sure, converting and confirming the soul and making wise the simple. Now, if this were all of the Lord's personal testimony concerning the word, we might be left in doubt. But fifty years or so after this, when churches had been multiplied, so that he could group them territorially or universally, he used the term some twenty times more. In Revelation he did not group the churches of Asia into the church of Asia, but he maintained the congregational idea both when he used the singular "church" and the plural "churches." It was as far from his idea to make one church of the seven as it was to make one star of the seven, or one candlestick of the seven; for how then could he walk in the midst of the candlesticks if there was only one? No more could he walk in the midst of the seven churches if they had been one; nor of the churches now, if they were one. "The seven candlesticks are the seven churches." After an address to each church, as to the church at Ephesus, to the church at Smyrna, etc., he closed each message with the exhortation, "He that hath an ear to hear, let him hear what the Spirit saith unto the churches." Even in the last chapter of Revelation we find in the sixteenth verse these words: "I, Jesus, have sent my angel to testify unto you these things in the churches." Now, out of these, say twenty-two instances of his use of the word, about half in the singular and half in the plural, on the ground that Christ's testimony always agrees with itself, are we not driven to the conclusion that in the first occurrence of the word there was the same conception in the divine mind as to what the church was to be that he would build? One instance out of twenty-three is a poor exception on which to build a universal church.

Chapter XVI.

We have the testimony of Jesus, "the true and faithful witness." He used the word church in Matthew and Revelation twenty-three times, and in twenty-two cases he used it in its usual congregational sense. No one will dispute that. Now, how can one persuade himself that in the first use he made of the word, when he spoke so specifically of building something on a sure foundation, and that no opposition, represented by descending rain, coming floods, blowing winds and gates of hades, beating upon it, should overthrow it; that he, in that specific use of the word, should have had a vague, undefined and undefinable sense, a sense that had never before been applied to the word, and which the Apostles could not have understood. They knew the quahal of the old Scriptures, and the sunagoge and ekklesia of the Septuagint, and now to boldly launch the same old familiar word with an entire new meaning upon the coming generations would doubtless have called for an explanation from the Apostles, as they tried to understand everything he taught, and seemed never to have hesitated to ask for explanations. Incredible! The idea of building something on a petra that would be assailed even by the gates of the unseen world, and yet should stand, and that something a nothing that could be or ever has been assailed, a something the word had never suggested, a something that he never suggested in his twenty-two other uses of the word; a something different from what was assailed, as we will soon see; a something that should receive the most violent opposition of anything else in all coming time, and yet should stand; a something that should be driven into the wilderness, and preserved in the dens and caves of the earth, and persecuted by the organized powers of the earth; a persecution that should last for 1,260 years by one power and then joined by others, and yet that persecuted something, called his church, was invisible and spiritual, unorganized and unofficered, without ordinances and doctrines; hence, without offense, would make the words of Christ false. No such a thing, or rather no such a nothing, has ever been assailed by any sort of visible powers. If Christ intended to reveal that he would build an invisible spiritual church, and that invisible spiritual powers would persecute his invisible spiritual members, and put them to death on account of their invisible spiritual doctrines, then he failed to reveal it, for this disciple of his can't conceive it or perceive it, and hence can't believe it. By reading Luke xxiii. 23 and Rev. xii. 7–8, etc., you will see that the word "prevail," as used concerning the church, indicates great effort, and history fully corroborates this. Shall not prevail against it—the church. Saul "persecuted the church," "made havoc of it," "persecuted it beyond measure," but he did not prevail. He scattered it, but that caused it to multiply. He did not persecute an invisible spiritual nothing, but the church at Jerusalem, because it had a "way" (Acts

xxii. 4); he tried to destroy its faith, and, finding he could not prevail, he went to preaching it himself (Gal. i. 23). Christ's church was destined to provoke opposition, to divide families, setting them at variance, even causing the dearest ones to put each other to death. Its mission was to turn and upturn and overturn worldly principles, practices, policies, polities, principalities and powers. It was not to be reformatory, but revolutionary. It was not to make compromises, but conquests. Old things must pass away and all things be made new. Christ had this mission of his church in mind when he said: "The gates of hades shall not prevail against it."

But let us seek further information and confirmation concerning the church Christ built. Every preacher at least once in his life, yea, every member, should follow the word in its every occurrence in the New Testament; yea, in the Old, and in all its secular use before it became so corrupted. Let us at least run briefly through the New Testament, and further if we have time. We will follow first the singular and then the plural, and save for the last those instances of its use where the universal idea is supposed to be conveyed.

No one has a right to use the word in an unscriptural sense, and can't without becoming a false witness of God; for we are to contend not only for sound words, but for their very form, yea, for their jots and tittles. "By thy words thou shalt be justified, and by thy words thou shalt be condemned."

By our words we influence others, and we are to be held responsible, and ought to be. Never was a word so used and abused, and if we have the faith once for all delivered, let us contend for it as first delivered, and yield nothing to modern demands. Christ's testimony is unmistakable.

But " the Holy Ghost is also a witness," and he was to bring to the apostles' minds all that Christ had commanded. So we find the apostles under the Spirit's guidance, both in writing and practice, establishing other churches after the model given, making each church complete in itself, and independent of all others. This we know was done. The nearly one hundred other usages of the word by the Holy Spirit through the apostles wonderfully confirm this view. So also the meaning of the word, and other like words and circumstances and other co-ordinate terms, make the other idea impossible to maintain. My mind could not rest with any other conclusion.

But let us go back and make another start. To whom did Christ give his commission? If to the individual disciples as such whom he addressed, then they must live to the end of the age. If to the apostles as such, then they would live to the end of the age, or would have successors to the end of the age. I think we are all agreed that he addressed them as constituting his church, and of that there should be no end. He commissioned the church to preach, to baptize, to teach and to keep safely all things delivered to the end of the age, with the promise of omnipresent omnipotence in all the days. Here is authority to do certain things. The church had no authority before this because the head of the church had not delegated it. He had taught them about these things, but they had not exercised themselves in them. Christ had directed the baptisms (John iv. 1) and the supper and the expulsion of Judas; but after waiting for enduement with power from on high they began the very work of preaching, baptizing, etc., that they were sent to do.

Were they to make disciples, baptize them and turn them loose in the world, or add them together in organized capacity? If the first, then we might regard them in some way as belonging to the universal church, and, if so, they belonged to that as soon as they were saved, and by virtue of being saved. But the Lord did not regard these saved persons as belonging to any church, and so we read Acts ii. 47: "The Lord added to the church daily the saved." If the church built on the rock is constituted of all the saved, then he added these church members to another church. Why have two churches so unlike? One visible, the other invisible? One local, the other unlocal? One with ordinances, the other with none? One with doctrine, the other none? I don't believe he had but one kind of a church then, and I don't believe he ever had but one kind. But this we are now investigating. Let us proceed. In Acts ii. 47 the church was the church of Jerusalem. In Acts v. 11, "fear came upon all the church," means the church at Jerusalem. This is fully expressed in viii. 1: "The church which was at Jerusalem. Chapter viii. 3, "Saul made havoc of the church," is the same thing. A persecution that arose on the death of Stephen scattered the thousands of members from Jerusalem throughout Judea, Samaria and Galilee, and thus the church was multiplied—that is, other churches were formed after the pattern at Jerusalem.

In xi. 22 we have again "the church which was at Jerusalem," and in verse 26 "they assembled with the church," which proves that the church was an assembly. In chapter xii. 1, Herod stretched forth his hand to vex certain of the church, (at Jerusalem) and seeing it pleased the Jews he took Peter also, which led the church (verse 5) to meet and pray without ceasing to God for Peter. This is all congregational so far. Chapter xiii. 1 says, " There were in the church that was at Antioch;" xiv. 23, "elders in every church;" xiv. 27, "gathered the church together." These are strong and to the point. Chapter xv. 3, "brought on their way by the church" (at Antioch); verse 4, "they were received of the church" (at Jerusalem). Here each of these is the church. In verse 22 the latter is called the whole church, which shows itself complete in itself; xviii. 22, "saluted the church" (at Cesarea); xx. 17, "called the elders of the church" (at Ephesus); Rom. xvi. 1, " servant of the church" (at Cenchrea); verse 5, "the church that is in their house;" verse 23, "the whole church [at Corinth] salute you."

1 Cor. i 2, " unto the church which is at Corinth;" iv. 17, "as I teach everywhere in every church;" vi. 4, "the least esteemed in the church;" x. 32, "give no offence to the church of God," means the church at Corinth; xi. 18, "when ye come together in the church;" xi. 22, "despise ye the church of God?" (In which the supper was being perverted.) Chapter xii. 28, " God set some in the church " (at Jerusalem, the last of which was diversities of tongues on the day of Pentecost). Chapter xiv. 4, " edifieth the church;" 5, " that the church may receive edifying;" 12, "to the edifying of the church;" 19, "I had rather speak in the church;" 23, " the whole church be come together;" 28, "keep silence in the church;" 35, "shame for a woman to speak in the church." Chapter xv. 19, " I persecuted the church of God " (at Jerusalem); xvi. 19, " the church that is in their house;" 2 Cor. ir 1, " the church of God which is at Corinth;" Gal. i. 13, "I persecuted the church of God " (at Jerusalem); Phil. v. 5, "concerning zeal, persecuting the church;" iv. 4, " no church [at any place] communicated with me;" Col. iv. 15, " the church in his house;" iv. 16, " read also in the church of the Laodiceans;" 1 Thess. i. 1, " unto the church of the Thessalonians;" 2 Thess, i. 1, " unto the church of the Thessalonians;" 1 Tim. iii. 5, " how shall he take care of the church of God" (in any place); iii. 15, " behave thyself in the house of God,

which is the church of the living God;" v. 16, "let not the church be charged;" Philem i. 2, "to the church in thy house;" Heb. ii. 12, " in the midst of the church will I sing praise" (fulfilled when Jesus sung a hymn and went out); Jas. v. 14, "call for the elders of the church" (the big church has no elders); John iii. 6, " borne witness of thy charity before the church;" 9, " I wrote unto the church;" 10, " casting them out of the church;" Rev. ii. 1, church at Ephesus; 8, church at Smyrna; 12, church at Pergamos; 18, church at Thyatira; 3, church at Sardis; 7, church in Philadelphia; 13, church of the Laodiceans.

In the above the congregational idea of the church is conceded, and can't be denied. We have tabulated more than half of the Bible occurrences of the word " church," and without a doubt they all so far sustain the congregational idea, and also forbid any other. We followed the word only in the singular number.

Now, is it not immensely significant that when the Holy Spirit would speak of more saints than a single congregation contains, instead of enlarging on, or departing from the congregational idea in the singular number, as is the almost universal custom, he preserves this idea by using the plural number? This he does thirty-six times. The first supposed occurrence of " churches" in Acts ix. 31 is very significant. King James has the plural and the late Revision the singular. The 3,000 of Acts ii. 41

added to the 5,000 "men" of Acts iv. 4, and these added to the great multiplication of disciples after the ordination of deacons in Acts vi. 7; and these with the "daily additions" of ii. 47, etc., constitute a number out of which many churches could be organized. These were all scattered from Jerusalem, except the apostles. There was some time between their dispersion and reorganization. Acts ix. 31 was after the dispersion, and if it was before the reorganization began, then the church which was at Jerusalem was scattered throughout Judea, Samaria and Galilee. But if the scattered disciples had at that time begun to organize in their several places of abode, which they certainly did at some time, then it should read "churches." In either case there is no collision with our doctrine, unless it can be shown that in another place the Holy Spirit designated a province or provinces, and then used the singular "church" to include the churches of that territory. But this cannot be shown. The Holy Spirit never mentioned a province or nation, and then used the singular church to include the churches of that territory. But in every other case he refused to do it, and so should we. But here is the plural list.

Acts xv. 41, "And he went through Syria and Cilicia, confirming the churches;" xvi. 5, "churches established;" Rom. xvi. 4, "churches of the Gentiles;" xvi. 16, "churches of Christ." If it were right to include all saints in one church of Christ, here was the place to do it. The Holy Spirit refused to do it, and so should we. He did not use "churches" to include a plurality of denominations, nor should we. He used churches to include a plurality of congregations, and so should we. 1 Cor. vii. 17, "so I ordain in all churches" (that is, congregations); 1 Cor. xi. 16, "cnurches of God." When the Holy Spirit refers to one he says church of God at Corinth, etc., but when he would include all the saints everywhere, he says churches of God, and so should we. In xiv. 33, "all churches of the saints;" 34, "Let your women keep silence in the churches." Let the women rejoice in this doctrine, for the universal church idea lays on them universal silence. If every one is in the church by virtue of her faith, and this church is without habitation or place of meeting, then women are as much in the church in their parlors and kitchens as in a house of worship. If it is a shame for a woman to speak in the church, and the church be universal and not congregational, then let not believing women speak anywhere, for they would always be in the church. In xvi. 1, "churches of Galatia;" xvi. 19, "churches of Asia;" 2 Cor. viii. 1, "churches of Macedonia;" 18, "throughout all the churches" (not church); 19, "chosen of the churches;" 23, ', messengers of the churches" (not church); 24, "before the churches;" xi. 8, "robbed other churches;" 28, "care of all the churches" (not church); xii. 13, "inferior to other churches" (congregations); Gal. i. 2, "churches of Galatia;" 22, "churches of Judea;" 1

Thess. ii. 14, "followers of the churches of God, which in Judea are in Christ Jesus;" 2 Thess. i. 4, "we glory in the churches of God" (not church); Rev. i. 4, "seven churches which are in Asia." These churches are referred to thirteen times in the first three chapters in the plural number and once in the 16th verse of the last chapter. Seven times in these first three chapters, Jesus Christ, who organized his church, and who at that time had been a long time in heaven, re-affirms the congregational idea by speaking of a congregation as THE CHURCH, and thirteen times in these chapters when he would enlarge on the idea of a congregation, he used the plural, churches. So we, whenever and wherever we use the term " the church," "the church of God," " the church of Christ," should refer to a congregation; and whenever and wherever we speak of more than a congregation, we should use the plural number.

We will next notice the passages which are supposed to refer to a universal church.

Chapter XVII.

There are passages of Scripture which, it is thought, justify the use of the term church in a universal, invisible, inorganic, incomprehensible, uncongregational sense. We are glad to concede that persons will be saved from all nations, kindreds, tongues and peoples, many of whom were never recognized as saved; never had any organic connection with the saved, but we see no Scripture or propriety in connecting them in this life with the church. "The saved were added to the church." This is proper when convenient, but they must be in a saved state first. The thief on the cross was saved out of the church; and so of all others. The saved ought to congregate, so as to work together for the Lord, but all do not, and we don't think the Scriptures justify us in extending the boundaries of the church so as to take all in. On the contrary we think the custom is unscriptural and fraught with evil, as it encourages persons to remain out of the church, thinking they are in, and then to make war on the true church.

But let us notice some of the places where the universal idea of the church is thought to be taught. Leaving for the present Matt xvi. 18, we turn to Acts xx. 28, " Feed the church of God which he has purchased with his own blood." The connection clearly settles this down into the congregational list. Paul, from Miletus, sent to Ephesus, and called for the elders of the church, and said among other things: " Take heed unto yourselves, and to all the FLOCK in which the Holy Spirit has made you bishops, to feed the church of God," etc. (Ox. Rev.) Christ purchased with his blood the church at Ephesus, which is the church of God, and this church of God was co-extensive with the " flock," or congregation, to which these elders were to give heed, and in which they were placed as bishops. Make it the universal church, and you have universal elders or bishops, and, also, a universal flock.

In Paul's letter to this church, he uses the term church nine times, and most of these are claimed on the universal list. Chapter i. 22 and Col. i, 18, 24 belong to a class, and we put them together: " Gave him to be head over all things to the church, which is his body." " He is the head of the body—the church." "For his body's sake, which is the church."

Here the terms church and body are synonymous, or one is a figure of the other. Christ is the head of this body, or church, and organized saints are members of that body, or church. The figure is not that of a body on all fours, but a human body which carries the head " OVER all things," and not under or on a level. The body that exalts itself above the head is a "beast," and the " Beast " did this when it thought to " change times and ordinances." It thus exalted itself above the head. Now, a human body is the likeness of Christ's church. In this body we see unity in diversity among its members. Services differing, like those of the hands, feet, eyes and ears, yet all working together, " fitly joined together and compacted, by that which every joint supplieth, according to the effectual working in the measure of every part, making increase of the body unto the building up of itself." This is inexplicable and inapplicable except to a congregation. These members of the human body are not only " joined together," and working together, but in full sympathy, " having the same care one for another," so no one can say to another, "I have no need of you." "Not one member, bnt many." "If all were one member [as bishops in the general conference], where were the body?" "But now are there many members but one body." The feeble and uncomely members are necessary, and ought to have more abundant honor, for God tempered the body together so there should be no schism, but that they should suffer, work and rejoice together. "Now ye [church of God at Corinth] are the body of Christ and members each in his part." 1 Cor. xii. There are many kinds of bodies, but only one that will do to represent Christ's spiritual body, or church. Look a little at the likeness. "Joined together"—congregation; one head—Christ; complete in itself—a body, or the body. The eyes "oversee," but do not lord it over the others; the tongue speaks, but never against the members; the hands strike, but not one of the members; the feet, the servant of all, and lowest of all— these all working together to execute, not the law of the hands or eyes, for these can make no laws, but in all their co-operative labor, they do the will of the head. When a body gets to making laws, it puts itself on an equality with the head, or exalts itself above the head, and thus shows itself the body of a beast. The figure of a human body is an argument in favor of congregationalism, so potent that flesh and blood, and principalities and powers, and rulers of the darkness of this world and spiritual wickedness in high places, can't answer. If all the human bodies were made into one body, and became a great image, like the one Nebuchadnezzar saw, some little stone might strike its toes and grind it to powder, or it might fall of its own weight; but organized as it is, on a small scale, each complete in itself, the human body becomes an institution which the gates of hades cannot prevail against. These gates may close on one every second, yet the multiplication is so rapid and widespread that the body as an organization is destined to ride the surging billows and land at last on the uttermost shores of time. "I speak concerning Christ and his church."

We are considering the human body as a figure of the church, or body of Christ. As the human body is a compact organization, so is the body or church of Jesus Christ. As a human body is complete in itself, so also is the body or church of Jesus Christ. As the members of the human body co-operate to execute the will of the head, so of the members of the body or church of Christ. As the human body has only one head, so of the body or church of Christ. As a human body is the human body, so also the body or church of Christ. As the human body, considered as an institution, cannot be destroyed from the earth, so also the body or church of Christ. As the human body, wonderfully made, is of divine origin, so also the body or church of Christ. As the human body is dependent on God for preservation, so also is the body or church of Christ. As the human body has been redeemed or bought with the blood of Christ, so also the body or church of Christ.

If it be urged that this congregational idea of the church, or body of Christ, and he the head of every such church, would make Christ many headed, and to avoid this, all congregations must be considered as one church, so Christ could be the one head of the universal body or church; then we must consider "every man" as one universal man, so Christ could be the head of the one big man. If the expresssion, "Christ is the head of every church," makes him multicapital, how much more the expression, "Christ is the head of every man." 1 Cor. xi. 3. But, as a universal man, in our present surroundings, is inconceivable, so is a universal church (congregation). As there can be no man without organic structure, so there can be no church. As universal organic structure in our present state is impossible in one case, so also in another.

Now, for the corollary to all this. If this be the true Scriptual idea of the church of Christ, then there is in it no scope for human ambition, and no authority to "lord it over God's heritage." This heavenly institution is sure death to popes, prelates, cardinals, archbishops, bishops, presiding elders, priests, presbyters, which John Miton says is but "priests written LARGE." Of course, he referred to dictatorial, authoritative presbyters. If this, the congregational church, is the church in Scripture, then it will be an easy matter to identify the church in history.

Before leaving this figure of a body, we ask you to refer to Rom. xii. 3-8, Eph. iv. 11-16 and 1 Cor. xi. 12-29, and you will see that it is a real, working local body, having offices, ordinances, practical duties and " a habitation and a name." By referring to 1 Cor. xii. 12, x. 17; Col, iii. 15, and Eph. iv. 3-7, you will see that there is only one body, and it an organization; so that, if we belong to that, we can't belong to any other. If the local organization is the body of Christ, then the universal idea is false, for there is only "one body," as an institution. "For as the [human] body is one, and hath many members, and all the members of that one [human] body, being many, are one [human] body, so also is Christ's [body]." The whole professing world (a few modern Baptists excepted), and also the Scriptures of divine truth, tell us that no unbaptized man is a member of this body, or church of Christ. See 1 Cor. xii. 13: " For in one Spirit were we all baptized unto one body, whether Jews or Gentiles, bond or free," etc. This Scripture tells us that a man must be in the Spirit when baptized, and Rom. viii. 9 tells us that " we are in the Spirit; if so be, the Spirit of God dwell in us." Eph. iv, 5 tells us that there is only one baptism, and since a man must be in the Spirit, or have the Spirit dwell in him before baptism, and AFTER this must be baptized, then the one baptism is water baptism; and since only immersion is water baptism, then it follows that only those who in the one Spirit were baptized—immersed—are in the one body. Now, those who in the one Spirit were called through the one baptism, unto the one body, subject to the one Lord, contending for the one faith, are exhorted, in all their intercourse with the members, to keep the unity of the Spirit in the bond of peace; acknowledging the "one God and Father of all as above all, and through all, and in all." This is the body or church of Scripture, the body or church of history, and the body or church which the gates of hades shall not prevail against. Christ is head over all things to this church, which is his body. (Eph. i. 22, 23.) Through this institution, the principalities and powers in heavenly places shall learn of the manifold wisdom of God. (Eph. iii. 10.) This is the institution which Christ built on a rock, and to which he gave judgment for the present age of all matters and members "within." (See Matt. xviii. 17, 1 Cor. v. 11 and 1 Pet. iv. 17.) But at last, when he shall gather them from the east and west, and north and south, into one "general assembly," or congregation of the first born ones, being all together with Christ, as at first ("for where he is there shall we be also"), then before this general ASSEMBLY, the nations shall be gathered, and "the saints shall judge the world," and "shall judge angels." (1 Cor. vi. 2, 3.) For this he built his church, for this he has preserved it, and to this he will ultimately bring it to the exceeding riches of his glorious grace. "Now, unto him who is able to do exceeding abundantly above all we can ask or think, according to the power that worketh in us, unto him be glory IN THE CHURCH, THROUGHOUT ALL AGES, world without end. Amen."

We must now dismiss "the body," as a figure of the church, with the sole remark that by no process of right reasoning, neither by analogy or Scripture, can this figure be used against the congregational idea. There are other figures that are wont to be pressed into "the universal" service that we will briefly notice. In Eph. v. 22–23 we have the relation existing between Christ and his church represented by the relation existing between the husband and the wife. The first point of resemblance is that of submission. "Wives, submit yourselves unto your own husbands as unto the Lord. For the husband is the head of the wife EVEN AS Christ is the head of the church; and he is the Savior of the body." As each particular husband is the head of each particular wife (see verse 23), even so is the (omnipresent) Christ the head of each particular church, just as he is the head of each particular man. "For I would have you know that the head of every man is Christ, and the head of every woman is the man." 1 Cor. xi. 3. As it is not necessary to convert these terms, "woman," "wife," "husband," "man," into a universal, invisible, inconceivable woman, wife, husband, man; so it is not necessary to convert each church (congregation) into a universal, invisible, inconceivable church (congregation). For AS is the one, SO is the other, says the Holy Spirit.

We believe the time is coming when all of these miniatures, models, embryos, types, figures, etc., will be done away. The local congregation, which is the present miniature, model, etc., having been set up through all the ages and through all the earth for men to SEE, will at last give way for " the general assembly and church of the first born," but at present we have to do only with the figure of the true. Let us learn the lesson assigned for the present age, by holding on to the prescribed institutions of this age, and thus qualify ourselves for the enlarged lessons of the future age. We do not indorse the idea of a present universal church (congregation). It can't be gotten out of the figures, body, woman, wife, bride, etc., for all of these are specific, tangible, comprehensible, visible, local. The same may be said of vine, family, building, temple, sheepfold, field, etc. Not one of these favor the idea of a universal church.

The idea of combining all the great variety of vines in this world into one grand, conglomerate, universal, invisible vine, and then become so enraptured with the hallucination that we ignore and despise all the visible, organic, specific ones, is, to us, on a par with the universal church theory. And so of the others. " Ye are God's building," " ye are God's field," was addressed to the church at Corinth. These are specific terms, and convey to our minds specific ideas, and to mystify them is to despise instruction.

But you have perhaps arrayed Eph. iii. 14 against all this. There seems to be the idea of a universal family. We have heard some of our liberal brethren soar aloft on this text. Every one in all ages saved by Christ constitute the divine family or church, say they. We reply, briefly, that God hath set every member in his (church) family as it hath pleased him, so that there be no divisions, so they can " all meet in one place" and have no schism or strife. But an experiment of this kind, with " all names," would make this divine family a family of Kilkenney cats. We don't believe the whole family (?) in heaven and earth is named for the Father of our Lord Jesus Christ. A correct translation would give another idea. The following is from Conybeare & Howson:

"From whom every fatherhood in heaven and earth is named, i. e., the very name refers us back to God as the father of all. The A. V. is incorrect."

Alford, Middleton, etc., translated "every family" instead of "whole family." So of the late Revision, which gives in the margin, "Greek, fatherhood." The apostle thus implies that God as a Father is the great prototype of the paternal relation whether found in heaven or on earth. In Eph. ii, 21 the language, "The whole building, fitly framed together, groweth unto a holy temple in the Lord," is changed likewise by the late Revision into "each several building." See also Broadus, Weston and Hovey, who support the above.

All this, with the general tenor of Scripture, ought to restrain our brethren from straining the word church out of its legitimate, common sense, Scripture usage. Read Jas. v. 19-20.

CAAPTER XVIII.

The God of heaven set up his kingdom subsequent to Daniel's prophecy. Its nigh approach was announced by John, its presence repeatedly asserted by Christ. Men and women entered it during Christ's ministry, and the violent tried to take it by force. This is the kingdom that should "stand forever," and that should "not be left to other people." It was the Father's good pleasure to give to the little flock this kingdom, and Christ delivered it to them in solemn trust. Daniel had said that "the saints of the most High should take the kingdom, and possess the kingdom forever, even forever and ever. The kingdom and dominion and greatness of the kingdom under the whole heavens should be given to the saints of the most high," and this kingdom was never to pass away. The dream "was Certain and the interpretation of it Sure."

This kingdom was to be spread by human effort, by making disciples and baptizing them. These baptized disciples were to co-operate in the extension of this kingdom. Hence they were to be organized in different places into ecclesiae. These called out and assembled people must be governed by right principles, for Christ constituted them his executors, or business—doing bodies. The bodies were local, because they were assemblies, and visible because composed of real saints. Christ organized one after which all others were to be patterned. This business—doing body he called his church, and these churches were to multiply themselves, and thus spread the kingdom. Each congregation was complete in itself, and independent of the others, and of civil government. These assemblies were and are distinguishable from all other congregations of men by their divine marks.

This "spiritual house" was to be built up of "spiritual stones to offer up spiritual sacrifices holy and acceptable unto God." No one, however rich or learned or honored, could rightly join it, until he was born again—must be saved before added to the church; hence they were called saints or holy ones—having been washed, sanctified, justified in the name of the Lord Jesus and in the Spirit of our God. All other congregations, assemblies, bodies, churches (?) admit the unsanctified, the unsaved, and hence they are unholy.

The second divine mark is the polity of fraternal equality. No one exercising authority upon, or lording it over the others. Christ emphatically declared that this should not be so with his disciples. The world never produced such a body, with such a polity, and it never saw but one, and that it hates.

Those so-called Congregationalists are counterfeits. They violate the very principles their name indicates, and thus they make void the commandment of Christ by their tradition—infant rantism.

The next mark is—this body is divided into three classes: saints, bishops and deacons, with the saints first in authority, because in majority, and the officers are the servants of the saints by virtue of their office. There is only one business—doing body in this world possessing this peculiarity—the greatest the slave of all; equal as a member but subordinate as an officer.

The mission of this church constitutes another divine mark. Her work is to make disciples—immerse them, and teach them all things whatsoever Christ has commanded. There is only one body observing this order, and doing this work and the work cannot be done except in order. It does not read, Go into all the world and sprinkle all the babies and teach the Catechism or Discipline. That is the commission of Pedo-baptists and is of men and contrary to God.

Another divine mark of this heavenly kingdom, and hence of the business—doing bodies composing is that, like its founder, it disdains all alliance with the kingdoms of this world. The god of this world offered all the kingdoms to Christ, but he spurned the offer. So his kingdom while in the world is not to be of the world, but separate from the world. Among all the aspirants to these honors, mark well the one, who in the faith has steadfastly refused every such overture.

But the golden mark of all marks is the principle that underlies the actions, and all the actions, of all her subjects. The underlying principle is a vital one, so much so that no action destitute of it can be acceptable to God. The principle is seen in the following: "First make the tree good and the fruit will be good." "A corrupt tree cannot bring forth good fruit, neither can a good tree bring forth evil fruit." "If ye love me keep my commandments." "If ye love me ye will keep my sayings." "He that loveth is (has been) born of God." "Every one that doeth righteousness is (has been) born of God." "Whosoever doeth not righteousness is not of God." "Whether ye eat or drink (or be baptized or eat the Lord's Supper) or whatsoever ye do, do all to the glory of God." "Herein is my Father glorified that ye bear much fruit; So shall ye be (not become) my disciples."

This divine principle is implanted in regeneration by the Holy Spirit and is necessary to acceptable obedience. All so-called outward obedience, rendered with a view to obtain forgiveness, salvation or acceptance with God, is obedience to "another gospel which is not another." It is antipodal to the gospel, and infinitely worse than no gospel, because it perverts the gospel of Christ. Hence we may expect under this mark to find the true church through the past ages denouncing the rite of infant rantism or immersion and other acts under the false principle as "inventions of the devil" and "subversive of the gospel of Christ." There are other distinguishing marks, but these are sufficient to identify the true church whenever and wherever found. Are these marks Scriptural? Do they characterize the church Christ said "I will build?" Have the gates of hades prevailed against it? It should afford us heavenly delight and spiritual pride and courage to champion the truth contained in these questions even in the face of a modern but widespread opposition.

Before we go into the polity of a church, which is one of its strongest marks of identification, let us emphasize the congregational feature of the church, which marks the limitation of its polity. The churches of Christ are congregational in a double sense: 1st, in limiting all authority to the congregation, and 2nd, in extending authority to all in the congregation. We long since gave up all fanciful notions of the church, and we never speak of it now, except in its congregational sense. We regard the ideal notions as unreasonable, unscriptural, and of evil tendency, and that to an alarming extent. These liberal notions that go beyond the congregational idea, accommodate every error in the world on the church question, and confirm nine-tenths of professing Christendom in any error they may entertain on the subject. If the Catholic universal idea of the visible church is correct, then it has all sorts of polities, all sorts of ordinances, all sorts of faiths, all sorts of characters, all sorts of divisions, etc., with no possible way to cleanse the augean stable. Or if the other idea, the invisible, be preferred, it has none of these things; no officers to serve, or rule, it never meets, and has no commission to do anything.

Congregationalism lays the axe to the root of the "holy Catholic church," and it is destined to hew it down and cast it into the fire. Dan. ii. 34–35; 44–45. The little stone must smite the great image, and make it like the chaff of the summer threshing floor, so that the wind carries it away till no place be found for it, before it becomes great and fills the whole earth. One mark of indestructibility which Christ put upon his church is congregationalism. The diabolical powers of hierarchical governments have been exhausted on congregationalism, and yet it lives. Make havoc of it in Jerusalem, and scatter the congregation throughout Judea, Samaria and Galilee, and the scattered members will congregate in the name of Christ, in their several places, and thus the church by persecution is multiplied, and "the blood of the martyrs becomes the seed of the church." Bring to bear against any hierarchy one thousandth part of the destructive opposition that for more than one thousand years was hurled at congregationalism, and it would be ground to powder. But let us return to the Scripture arguments.

We propose now to give the characteristics of a true church from the Holy Scriptures, so that we may be able to distinguish it through the ages. See the underlying principles of church government as enunciated by Christ in the following:

Matt. xxiii. 8-12: "But be not ye called Rabbi: for one is your Master, even Christ; and all ye are brethren. And call no man your father upon the earth: for one is your Father, which is in heaven. Neither be ye called masters: for one is your Master, even Christ. But he that is greatest among you shall be your servant. And whosoever shall exalt himself shall be abased; and he that shall humble himself shall be exalted."

Mark states it thus: Mark x. 35-45: "And James and John, the sons of Zebedee, come unto him, saying, Master, we would that thou shouldest do for us whatsoever we shall desire. And he said unto them, What would ye that I should do for you? They said unto him, Grant unto us that we may sit, one on thy right hand, and the other on thy left in thy kingdom. And when the ten heard it, they began to be much displeased with James and John. But Jesus called them to him, and saith unto them, Ye know that they which are accounted to rule over the Gentiles exercise Lordship over them; and their great ones exercise authority upon them. But so shall it not be among you: but whosoever will be great among you, shall be your servant. And whosoever of you will be the chiefest, shall be the slave (doulos) of all. For even the Son or man came not to be served, but to serve, and to give his life a ransom for many."

Luke is a little clearer still: "And there was also a strife among them, which of them should be accounted the greatest. And he said unto them, The kings of the Gentiles exercise lordship over them; and they that exercise authority upon them are called benefactors. But ye shall not be so: but he that is greatest among you, let him be as the younger; and he that is chief, as he that doth serve. For whether is greater, he that sitteth at meat, or he that serveth? is not he that sitteth at meat? but I am among you as he that serveth."

See this sentiment inculcated by Peter in his first Epistle, fifth chapter: "The elders which are among you I exhort, who am also an elder, and a witness of the sufferings of Christ, and also a partaker of the glory that shall be revealed: Feed the flock of God which is among you, taking the oversight thereof, not by constraint, but willingly; not for filthy lucre, but of a ready mind; Neither as being lords over God's heritage, but being ensamples to the flock. And when the chief Shepherd shall appear, ye shall receive a crown of glory that fadeth not away. Likewise, ye younger, submit yourselves unto the elder. Yea, all of you be subject one to another, and be clothed with humility: for God resisteth the proud, and giveth grace to the humble"

See also Rom. xii. 10; 1 Cor. xvi. 15, 16; Gal. v. 12-14; Eph. v. 21. There is no passion in man so strong as his ambition for lordship, or rule, or authority over his fellows. Zebedee's family illustrates this principle. For pre-eminence, man will sacrifice weal, wealth, wine and woman. Hence the importance of divine teaching on this subject. Hence the divine teaching is not of the earth earthy, but is from heaven. "Whosoever would be great among you must be your diakonos and whosoever of you will be chiefest shall be doulos of all." Official subordination to fraternal equality is a mark of the divine institution called the church. Any claimant to church honors must not have officers in authority, for Christ has said "it shall not be so with you." Now who will say, it has been so, is now, and shall be in the church of Christ?

Nor will it do to say that principles of government are matters of minor importance. Whoever says so, deceives himself, and may deceive others. No kingdom of this world ever thought so. Whether the government adopted be a monarchy, limited, or absolute, or whether it be an aristocracy or democracy, the government adopted is always regarded as of the utmost importance.

This is equally true when we come to those claiming church honors. The Papacy would indicate their principles of government in their very name, and assert them in their teaching with unmistakable certainty and untiring frequency.

The Episcopalians would have you know by their very name the importance they attach to the principles of church government. So of the Presbyterians, Congregationalists, etc. These names bespeak church government. The Methodists attach such importance to this doctrine that they would have us recognize them as the Methodist Episcopal Church, the Methodist Episcopal Church, South. Their idea of church government is incorporated in their name. Congregational Methodists is another branch testifying to the importance of church government. The Papacy copies after worldy monarchies, while the others copy after worldly aristocracies. The divine principles of government thrust into these institutions would prove fatally revolutionary. Of course it is a shame for Congregationalists or Independents to claim the principle of equality of all, while they withhold church privileges and ordinances from a large part of their members—infants and children. Let us take up this matter of church government in detail, and get the Scripture marks clear in our minds. This will enable us to identify it from rival claimants in all the days that are past and "to the end of the age."

Chapter XIX.

One of the basest sentiments ever impressed on the renewed mind by the serpentine trail of Satan's wiles and devices may be discovered in this expression: " Just so I am saved I am satisfied." What selfishness! What ignorance! What madness! What depravity! What are we saved for? To what are we saved, as well as from what? The unutterable torments of the damned from which we are saved are of no greater consideration than the inconceivable glories, honors and rewards to which and for which we are saved. All things are ours, and for our sakes. What for? To be used. How? Now is the time to learn and to prepare to fulfil our high destiny in the everlasting kingdom "under the whole heavens." "From faith to faith." "From grace to grace." "From glory to glory." This is the "course" in the heavenly college. Christ came that we might have life, and that we might have it more abundantly. What life? All life. Physical, mental, social, moral, spiritual and eternal life. Life more abundantly than the material kingdom—the mountains, moon, sun, stars and skies; for all these are to wax old and decay, while our years will fail not. Life more abundantly than the vegetable kingdom; more than the animal. Life more abundant than we ever had—have now or will have a hundred, a thousand, a million years hence—ten thousand streams of life ever pouring into life, and yet life never full. Ever widening, ever deepening, ever rising, everlasting life—the life of God. And what for? Why this heirship of God and joint heirship with Christ? If the saints are to possess all things and rule the nations, and judge the world and angels, had they not better now, in their present school of training, be exercising themselves in all knowledge of government and judgment? If judgment does not now begin at the house of God, where we can learn and practice judgment, what ineffable fools would we be sitting on Christ's throne and trying to handle the reigns of universal empire? If we don't learn and exercise judgment now, how can we be trusted to judge the world and angels? I don't believe Christ will trust those honors to those who were satisfied to be saved only, and who rejected and disdained the teaching and discipline necessary to prepare them for such responsibilities. Paul writing to the church at Philippi, chap. i. 9, 10, says: "And this I pray, that your love may abound yet more and more in all knowledge and judgment; that ye may approve things that are excellent," or "that ye may distinguish things that differ" (B., H. and W.) "in order that ye may be sincere and inoffensive (eis) as regards the day of Christ." Look at it again. Paul prays that our love for knowledge and judgment may increase more and more, that we may exercise ourselves in discerning things that differ. What for? Looking to the day of Jesus Christ when we shall reign with him as kings on the earth, ruling over cities and judging the nations in righteousness. I believe that all of the "satisfied to be saved" who submit their wills to the godly wills (?) of their superiors here will have it to do there, as He will have no use for idiots on the throne. Crowns and thrones are for kings, and kings have authority and must have subjects to rule. Crowns must be won, and must be won lawfully. The best developed in knowledge and judgment here will rule over the greatest cities and will have the greatest honors there.

These remarks are intended to stimulate your thirst for the knowledge of the principles of government, especially ecclesiastical government, as these are the principles ordained for discipline and development for the future purposes of His grace.

Having seen that the church is congregational and complete in itself, and independent of outside jurisdiction, with Christ for its only head and the Holy Spirit and the Holy Word for its guide, let us learn, first, how it is to

RECEIVE MEMBERS.

Rom. xiv. 1-4: "Him that is weak in the faith receive; not for decisions of disputes. One believes that he may eat all things; but he that is weak eats herbs. Let not him that eats despise him that eats not; and let not him that eats not judge him that eats; for God received him. Who art thou that judgest another's servant? To his own lord he stands or falls. But he shall be made to stand; for the Lord is able to make him stand." The question here was about receiving heathen converts who had not been entirely converted from all of their heathen superstitions. The instructions are to receive them, though weak in the faith, for God had received them. Teaching them all things Christ had commanded later on would correct the other errors, and this was to be done after receiving them. But who was to receive them? Presiding elder? Presbytery? Elders? Deacons? No! The church at Rome, composed of "all the beloved of God called saints." As there must be fellowship among all the members, and as fellowship can't be coerced, the introduction of a new member must be left to those who are to extend fellowship. Our custom is to receive one for baptism and church membership at the same time, and we ought to know about his fitness for both. If he has believed to the saving of his soul, then he has repented, and if he has repented, then he has been convicted of sin; and all of this implies an experience, and by the experience we judge of his fitness for baptism and church membership.

Do the Scriptures teach that a man must be convicted, must "sorrow," "mourn," "repent" "pray," "agonize," "believe," "love," etc., before baptism? Then let those who can hinder baptism inquire for this inward preparation, demand the fruits, and refuse or accept the candidate, according to the testimony he is able to give concerning his preparation. If these spiritual characteristics, with their fruits and effects, are required by the Scriptures, before baptism (and who will deny it?), and if it is by these that we are to know and be known, and if these are to be made known by the candidate, and if the Bible way for him to do this is by confession, it follows that when he is through with the evidences that go to establish his fitness, he will have related what is commonly known and ridiculed as an " experience." Again, since all these characteristics required for baptism are internal, and hence experimental, it follows that the candidate cannot make any of them known except by telling his experience. If he has been convicted and sorrowed to repentance, and is changed in mind, it is experimental, and he only knows it; and he can't make others know it without telling his experience. If he believes, he " has the witness in himself." Hence the possession of it is experimental, and peace and other fruits of it are likewise experimental. Hence he cannot make known his faith without telling his experience. If any one prays an acceptable prayer, " the prayer of faith," and knows that God has heard him, and that " he has the petition that he desired of him," then this, too, is a matter of experience, and can't be told without telling an experience. We can't make known that we have passed from death unto life by our love for the brethren without telling our experience. If one has such an experience, he ought to tell it, or he ought to write it, and have others to tell it for him. On any proper occasion and in all proper ways let him say, " Come and hear, all ye that love the Lord, and I will tell you what he has done for my soul."

Now if it is right to relate an experience at all, it is right to relate what is required before baptism, especially to him, or them, who may have the administration and guardian care of the ordinance. If the authority to administer be of man, let him tell it to the man; and if it be of the church, let him tell it to the church.

Mr. Alexander Campbell, who perhaps contributed more than any other man to this lax custom of receiving members, wrote a strong protest in the Millennial Harbinger, vol. 3, pp. 323-325. We give a few extracts:

"If there be no right of refusal, there is no right of choice; for he that dares not refuse, in any case, an applicant for immersion, has no choice, and consequently needs to exercise no judgment in the matter; he ought to baptise all applicants without question or demur, whether they be drunk or sober, sincere or hypocritical—of good or bad report. John the Baptist also refused applicants to his baptism on the ground of insincere repentance. Where grounds of suspicion present themselves, I cannot conscientiously proceed. No person ought to be introduced into a church, any more than into a family, without the consent of its members, especially if his admission should even endanger the removal of a well-tried, excellent brother or break up the communion of the brotherhood. This would be to plant a 'root of bitterness' in the church rather than pluck it out, as Paul commanded."

If a church should judge of the disqualifications of a member with reference to exclusion, then it should judge of the right qualifications of an applicant with reference to reception. In either case the judgment must be expressed by vote.

"Receive ye." The ye is the church, and the church satisfying itself that the Lord has received him, is ready to extend fellowship as to a child of God. How they decided the matter is easily learned from other cases where the church gave expression of her judgment.

The same authority that receives members is necessary to their

EXCLUSION.

We find in Matt. xviii. 15–18 that the church excludes, binds and looses, and the church means the congregation. In 1 Cor. v. 4, 5, 12, 13 we have a case of penal discipline that throws all the needed light on the subject. Note well that the "ye" who exercised the discipline is "the church at Corinth," not the pastor or the deacons or a board of elders, but the "whole church" (xiv. 23) assembled in one place.

Barnes, the great Presbyterian, in his preface, p. xi., says: "The act of discipline which he had required on the incestuous person was to be inflicted by the whole congregation." In his note, p. 107, he says further: "The exercise of discipline belongs to the church itself. The church....was to remove the offender. Even Paul an apostle, and the spiritual father of the church, did not claim the authority o remove an offender except through the church

The church was to take up the case, to act on it, to pass the sentence, to excommunicate the man. There scarcely could be a stronger proof that the power of discipline is in the church.... If Paul would not presume to exercise such discipline,.... surely no minister, and no body of ministers, have any such right.... Every church is itself to originate and execute all the acts of discipline over its members."

Lyman Coleman says: "The discipline of the apostolic churches was administered by each body of believers collectively, and continued to be under their control until the third or fourth century. About this period the simple and efficient discipline of the primitive church was exchanged for a complicated and oppressive system of penance administered by the clergy." (Primitive Church, p. 87).

Canon Litton says: "The most important of the rights which belong to the laity relates to the exercise of discipline. That the power of inflicting church censures is to be vested not in the clerical body alone, but in the whole church, rests on the clearest evidence of Scripture. The final court of appeal which our Lord, speaking by anticipation, establishes in cases of disagreement among Christians, is the church; i. e., the whole congregation; conferring at the same time upon the church the power of enforcing its decrees by the penalty of excommunication." (Church of Christ, p. 405).

Dean Stanley says: "It is as sure that nothing like modern episcopacy existed before the close of the first century, as it is that nothing like modern Presbyterianism existed after the beginning of the second. That which was once the Gordian knot of theologians has at last in this instance been untied' not by the sword of persecution, but by the patient unravelment of scholarship." (Christian Institutions, p. 172).

In 2 Cor. ii. 6–8 we find this man was excluded by the majority, and the church is exhorted to restore the penitent lest he be swallowed up with overmuch sorrow.

Chapter XX.

Having noted the autonomy of the church in Receiving, Excluding and Restoring members, we come next to the election of officers. We will begin with the temporary officers. Of these we find in the Scriptures two, Messengers and Apostles. Epaphroditus was a messenger of the church at Philippi (Phil. 1. 25), but we are not told how he was chosen. To determine this we turn to 2 Cor. viii. 16–19, 23–4: "But thanks be to God, who puts the same diligence for you into the heart of Titus. For he accepted indeed our exhortation; but being very zealous, he went forth to you of his own accord. And together with him we sent the brother, whose praise in the gospel is throughout all the churches; and not that only, but who was also appointed by the churches, as our fellow-traveler with this gift which is administered by us, to further the glory of the Lord, and our zeal." "As to Titus, he is my partner, and in regard to you a fellow-worker; as to our brethren, they are messengers of the churches, the glory of Christ. Therefore show toward them before the churches, the proof of your love, and of our glorying on your behalf." Whether Titus was a messenger or general missionary agent, or whether the brother sent with him was the same or something different, and whether these two constituted "the brethren" styled "the messengers of the church," matters nothing in the discussion of this question. Whether these or others can or can not be identified, there were temporary officers chosen of the churches, and our enquiry is, How was it done? Were they appointed by a ruler or presbytery, or were they chosen of the churches? The Scripture quoted settles that. How was it done? We will let others speak for us. Schaff says, p. 509: "The officers and also delegates for special purposes (2 Cor. viii. 18, 19; Acts xv. 2) were taken from the midst of the congregation and were chosen by the people themselves." Scott says: "It may here again be observed that there is not the least reason to doubt but that the messengers . . . . were chosen by the suffrage of the churches." Whitby remarks in v. 17 touching the underlying principle of autonomy: "Of his own accord." Here we see the sweet harmony there is betwixt the grace of God and our persuasion and free will. Titus was moved to the work by Paul's exhortation and was also willing of his own accord, and yet "God," saith the apostle, "put this earnest care into his heart." How can God working in lead us to work out if men have the government over us? What does a ruling bishop care for God working in the heart of a preacher to serve a certain church, and in the church to have such a service? I know a preacher who plead such an inward working as a reason why he should preach and labor in a certain field, and the presiding elder told him he was not to preach where he preferred, but where his superiors sent him. This opened his eyes and he soon discovered the divine church government, and is now rejoicing in the liberty wherewith Christ has set him free, and is no longer under such a yoke of bondage.

But we must pass to the next point, to the election of Matthias to fill the vacancy made by the deposition and subsequent death of Judas. Acts i. 14–17, 21–26: "These all continued with one accord in prayer, with [certain] women, and Mary the mother of Jesus, and with his brothers. And in those days Peter stood up in the midst of the brethren, and said (and there was a multitude of persons together, about a hundred and twenty): Brethren, it was necessary that the Scripture should be fulfilled, which the Holy Spirit through the mouth of David spoke before concerning Judas, who became guide to those who took Jesus. Because he was numbered among us, and obtained the allotment of this ministry."

"It is necessary therefore, that of the men, who accompanied us all the time that the Lord Jesus went in and out among us, beginning from the immersion of John, to the day when he was taken up from us, of these one become a witness with us of his resurrection. And they set forth two, Joseph called Barsabas, who was surnamed Justus, and Matthias. And they prayed, and said, Thou, Lord, who knowest the hearts of all, show which of these two thou didst choose, that he may take the place in this ministry and apostleship, from which Judas by transgression fell away, that he might go to his own place. And they gave lots for them; and the lot fell upon Matthias; and he was numbered with the eleven apostles." Who were the "they" that voted in v. 26? Evidently the hundred and twenty, and that included the women. It can be settled by grammar as well as by Scripture. If a vote is ever to be taken from the church, it seems that this was the place to do it. Who are better qualified than inspired apostles to select and elect one to their office? But they had been taught better. What a nice presbytery they would have made to act for the church. But the ascended Redeemer of his people and church did not want any presbytery usurping the authority of his church. Why didn't Peter, the pastor, bishop or pope, appoint the successor of Judas? The answer is plain. He had been with Jesus, and had been taught of him. But let others holding to different views testify to the word of truth:

Schaff, p. 501, says: "So soon as there was a community of believers, nothing was done without its active participation.... Peter here lays before the whole congregation of about one hundred and twenty souls the necessity of an election to complete the sacred number twelve. Whereupon not only the apostles, but the whole body of disciples nominate Joseph Barsabas, and Matthias as candidates; all pray to be informed of the divine will (v. 24); all cast their lots, and thus Matthias is elected. Much more must we expect the general rights of Christians to be regarded in the choice of the ordinary congregational officers."

Comp. Comt. says: "The hundred and twenty did so, for to them Peter spake, and not to the eleven."

J. F and Brown: "Not the eleven, but the whole company....was numbered—voted on by general suffrage."

Jacobus: "Not the apostles who did this, but the whole assembly whom Peter addressed. It is clear that the membership were held to be on an equal footing in regard to their vote or lot here. The same entire body of members pray and cast their lots."

In Rev. ii. 2 we see that the church at Ephesus "Tried them which say they are apostles and are not, and found them to be liars." If the church did not depose them, it at least exposed them. This verifies the statement that " the apostles were put in the church," and that the church had "judgment on those that were within."

We now come to the permanent officers in the church. The first record of an election is that of Deacons. Acts vi. 1-6: "And in these days, when the number of the disciples was multiplying, there arose a murmuring of the Grecian Jews against the Hebrews, because their widows were overlooked in the daily ministration. And the twelve called the multitude of the disciples to them, and said, It is not proper that we should leave the word of God, and minister to tables. But, brethren, look ye out among you seven men of good repute, full of the Spirit and of wisdom, whom we will appoint over this business. And we will give ourselves to prayer and to the ministry of the word. And the word pleased the whole multitude. And they chose Stephen, a man full of faith and of the Holy Spirit, and Philip, and Prochorus, and Nicanor, and Timon, and Parmenas, and Nicolas a proselyte of Antioch, whom they set before the apostles; and having prayed, they laid their hands on them." These deacons were not appointed by one man, nor by the twelve inspired apostles, but elected by the whole church. The proposition pleased the whole multitude (including the women), and they (the whole multitude) chose the seven, whom they set before the apostles for ordination.

Schaff says: "When the first deacons are to be appointed (Acts vi.) the twelve call together the multitude of disciples and require them to make a choice. The latter fall in with the proposition, make their own choice, and present the candidates to the apostles, not for confirmation, but only for ordination."

Jacobus says: "The body of the members here make the election.... The rights of the people were held sacred.... How easy for the apostles to have assumed the absolute and undivided rule, with no reference to the popular element. Yet they were far from such a usurpation in the church of Christ. ....It was done by the church—apostles and members jointly.... They unanimously concurred in the direction of the apostles and proceeded accordingly."

The expression in v. 3—" whom we may appoint over this business" the word for appoint (kathisteemi) is the one translated ordain in Titus i. 5—"ordain elders in every city"—and in Heb. v. 1—"high priest is ordained for men"—and in viii. 3—" every high priest is ordained to offer," etc. It refers to the ceremony in v. 6 of praying and laying on of hands. The apostles constituted the ordaining presbytery, while the church elected those it preferred, and set them before the apostles for ordination and not for their appointment.

Neander says: "It is evident that the first deacons and the delegates who were authorized by the church to accompany the apostles, were chosen from the general body.... From these examples we may conclude that a similar mode of proceeding was adopted at the appointment of presbyters."

We will consider the election of presbyters the next time. We close this with the following from Gibbon's Rome, Vol. l., pp. 554-ff. An infidel writer is supposed not to be biased on ecclesiastical questions.

"The government of the church has often been the subject as well as the prize of religious contention. The hostile disputants of Rome, of Paris, of Oxford and of Geneva have alike struggled to reduce the primitive and apostolic model to the respective standards of their own policy.... The scheme of policy, which under their approbation was adopted for the use of the first century, may be discovered from the practice of Jerusalem, of Ephesus, or of Corinth. The societies which were instituted in the cities of the Roman empire were united only by the ties of faith and charity. Independence and equality formed the basis of their internal constitution.... The primitive bishops were considered only as the first of their equal and the honorable servants of a free people. Whenever the episcopal chair became vacant by death, a new president was chosen among the presbyters by the suffrages of the whole congregation, every member of which supposed himself invested with a sacred and sacerdotal character. Such was the mild and equal constitution by which the Christians were governed more than a hundred years after the death of the apostles. Every society formed within itself a separate and independent republic, and although the most distant of these little States maintained a mutual as well as friendly intercourse of letters and deputations, the Christian world was not yet connected by any supreme authority or legislative assembly. ....The institution of synods was so well suited to private ambition and to public interest that in the space of a few years it was received throughout the whole empire.... As the legislative authority of the particular churches was insensibly superceded by the use of councils, the bishops obtained by their alliance a much larger share of executive and arbitrary power; and as soon as they were connected by a sense of their common interest, they were enabled to attack with united vigor the original rights of their clergy and people. The prelates of the third century imperceptibly changed the language of exhortation into that of command, scattered the seeds of future usurpations and supplied by Scripture allegories and declamatory rhetoric their deficiency of force and of reason. They exalted the unity and power of the church as it was represented in the Episcopal Office, of which every bishop enjoyed an equal and undivided portion."

Chapter XXI.

Having seen that the Messengers and Apostle Matthias and the Deacons were elected to their several offices by the suffrage of the whole church, we come now to examine the manner of election to the office of Elders or Presbyters or Bishops, all of which titles refer to the same order of persons. Acts xiv. 23: "And when they had ordained them elders in every church, and had prayed with fasting, they commended them to the Lord, on whom they believed." Our investigation leads us to ask how this was done. Again we are happy to have those who differ from us testify in our favor, though they do it against their own practice.

Schaff says, p. 501: "As to the presbyter bishops, Luke informs us (Acts xiv. 23) that Paul and Barnabas appointed them to the office in the newly founded congregation by taking the vote of the people, thus merely presiding over the choice. Such at least is the original and usual sense of cheirotonesantes." (Comp. 2 Cor. viii. 19).

Adam Clark says: "I believe the simple truth to be this, that in ancient times the people chose by the cheirotonia (lifting up of the hands), their spiritual pastor. The elders were appointed by Paul and Barnabas, but in the usual way of appointing officers—by the suffrages of the people. This mode of election by the whole body of the church remained unimpaired in the third century."

The word "ordained" means that Paul took the suffrages of the people as to whom they would have to be their elders. The Greek word is defined by Thayer: "To vote by stretching out the hand." Litton, a scholarly Episcopalian, says: "In locating ministers in the newly planted churches of Asia, Paul and Barnabas took the suffrages of the people, and in this way ordained them elders in every church, conceding to each society the power of selection, but reserving to themselves the right of approval and institution." (Church of Christ, p. 404).

The Didache (Teaching of the Twelve Apostles) has precisely the same word where it reads: "Elect therefore for yourselves bishops and deacons." (Ch. 15). Clement of Rome says: "The ministry were appointed with the consent of the whole church." (1st Epis. ch. 44). The Constitutions read: "Chosen by the whole people." (Book 8). The canons of the church of Alexandria say: "A bishop should be elected by the people." (Can. 2). Mosheim very justly says: "In those primitive times each Christian church was composed of the people, the presiding officers and the assistants or deacons. These must be the competent parts of every society. The principal voice was that of the people, or of the whole body of Christians; for the apostles themselves inculcated by their example that nothing of any moment was to be done or determined upon but without the knowledge and consent of the brotherhood." (Vol. i., p. 68). Dean Stanley says: "Bishops and presbyters alike were chosen by the whole mass of the people by show of hands." (Christian Inst., p. 175). Clement of Rome, close of first century, says in his first epistle to the Corinthians that the apostles appointed bishops and deacons with the concurrence of the whole church. Even the Roman Catholic Dollinger says in his History of the Church: "The election of the clergy could not canonically take place without the participation of the assembled community.... They chose the seven whom the apostles ordained.... The bishop in particular....was chosen by the voices of the brethren." (Vol. i., p. 242). Cyprian in the third century contended that the right of popular election is a principle sanctioned by the sacred Scriptures and based jure divino.

These quotations might be extended indefinitely. They cover a wide range and are sufficient to establish us in the truth of this Distinguishing Baptist Doctrine. But the question may be asked, How can great men like these testify so positively to a truth and then practice differently? As this involves not only a Distinguishing but a Peculiar Baptist doctrine, this is a good point to consider it. We will let some of these great men speak for themselves. Schaff says, p. 24: "The constitution of the church, like its doctrines, has an unchangeable substance, but a changeable form." The mission of the Baptists is to deny this. These men testify to the practice of immersion by the apostles and early Christians, but say that baptism has a changeable form and they proceed to change it. Protestants brought this heresy from Rome. The Catholic Bible (Douay) says on Matt. iii. 6 that baptism was by immersing or by dipping or plunging under water, and then adds: "But the church which cannot change the least article of the Christian faith is not so tied up in matters of discipline and ceremonies. Not only the Catholic Church, but also the pretended reformed churches have altered this primitive custom in giving the sacrament of baptism, and now allow of baptism by pouring or sprinkling water upon the person baptized."

So Calvin says (Christian Religion, xv. 19): "Whether the person who is baptized be wholly immersed, and that thrice or once, or be only sprinkled with water poured on matters very little; but that on account of the diversity of countries ought to be free to the churches, although it is certain both that the word itself of baptizing signifies to immerse, and that the rite of immersing was observed by the ancient church." Neither Catholics nor Protestants think they ought to keep the ordinances as delivered, but the churches (?) ought to be free to change the forms to suit themselves or countries. What do Protestants care for the Lord's Supper as first delivered? Christ's example of partaking with only the apostles—the church and his mother left out—is contrary to their sentiment of communing with one another, and so it is so much the worse for the example. The same is true of their attitude toward church government.

Mosheim, a Lutheran, after minutely describing the form of church government by the apostle on p. 20, uses this strange language: "If, however, it be true that the apostles acted by divine inspiration, and in conformity with the commands of their blessed Master, and this no Christian can call in question, it follows that the form of government which the primitive churches borrowed from that of Jerusalem, the first Christian assembly, established by the apostles themselves, must be esteemed as of divine institution. But from this it would be wrong to conclude that such a form is immutable and ought to be invariably observed, for this a great variety of events may render impossible.

The mission of Baptists is to hold fast all things whatsoever Christ has commanded, and that includes the forms even of sound words, and especially of sound doctrine. Read that last clause again. That "But" is the butt of a goat, the butt of the beast with seven heads and ten horns. It is the butt that has butted Baptists since the beginning. The Baptists have always filed their buts against these anti-Christian butts. Baptists say "but" the Lord ordained it thus, as you yourselves testify. Protestants and Catholics say, "but" we are not bound in things we esteem non-essential, especially the forms. Baptists say "but" the Lord commands nothing that is non-essential. Catholics and Protestants say "but" our canons and rulers judge differently. Baptists say but we have no canon but the Bible and no ruler but the Lord. Catholics and Protestants say but if you don't stop filing your buts, we will multiply and intensify ours with a double t. Many Baptists in these days can stand a but with one t, but two are too many.

The Methodist Discipline (1883, pp. 25, 26), reads: "It is not necessary that rites and ceremonies should in all places be the same, or exactly alike; for they have been always different, and may be changed according to the diversity of countries, times and men's manners.... Every particular church may ordain, change, or abolish rites and ceremonies, so that all things be done to edification."

The Episcopal translator of Mosheim, Dr. McClain, says in a note, p. 21: "The truth is, that Christ, by leaving this matter undetermined, has left to Christian societies a discretionary power of modeling the government of the church in such a manner as circumstantial seasons of times, places, etc., may require; and therefore, the wisest government of the church is the best and most divine; and every Christian saint has a right to make laws for itself, provided that these laws be consistent with charity and peace and with the fundamental doctrines and principles of Christianity." Of course these provisos are all provided by their own providence.

McGarvey, a disciple of A. Campbell, says in his notes in Acts i. 26: "Whether the selection of these two was made by the whole body of the disciples, or by the apostles alone, it is unimportant to determine. The case does not, as many have supposed, furnish a precedent on the subject of popular election of church officers."

And so it goes. Men invent something they like better than what Christ ordained, and then they hunt an excuse for making the substitution. And why do they do this? Because they claim the right to invent churches (?), and of course they must differ from other churches (?), and to make them differ they must claim the right to diversify the doctrines by changing what they call the forms. But they don't stop with forms. The change of subjects to infants and sinners was as sure death to the substance as sprinkling was to the form of baptism. To admit the principle of liberty to change is fatal to sound doctrine and church perpetuity. Let all the world know that these differences do not result from difficulties in interpreting the word, but from the arrogant presumptions of man to change the divine law to suit themselves and the seasons.

But let us return to the quotation from Dr. Schaff, with which we begun, and see if he does not acknowledge that his own church government was the invention of John Calvin and he tries to justify him in it:

"The constitution of the church, like its doctrines, has an unchangeable substance and a changeable form.... The latter varies with the necessities of the time, and with the particular circumstances. At first we find the apostolic constitution where the apostles are the infallible teachers and leaders of the church. In the second century the Episcopal system appears, which grows naturally into the metropolitan and patriarchal forms. The Eastern churches stop with the latter, while the Latin church in the

Middle Ages concentrates all the patriarchal power in the Roman bishop and develops the papal system. This degenerates at last into an intolerant spiritual despotism, when the Reformation produces new forms of church constitution, corresponding better with the free spirit of Protestantism, in particular the Presbyterian form of government, with lay representation." (Schaff, 24).

Let us rest and ruminate.

CHAPTER XXII.

At this point is perhaps the best place to consider a few questions that may give you trouble in your ministry and maybe in your minds. Before considering the Scripture involved, let us consider the nature of the troubles mentioned. The Campbellites in trying to proselyte uninformed Baptists generally do it by lessening the differences between them and us. Church government is one of the doctrines often claimed as one of agreement. The Campbellites are Congregationalists in one sense only, and that is, they have no authority outside of the congregation. That is, they limit the authority to the congregation, but their great error is in not extending authority to all in the congregation. Their government is a congregational episcopacy. They use the same terms the Presbyterians use, but the difference is this: While they both are governed by "ruling elders," with the Presbyterians the elders are composed partly of laymen, while all the Campbellite elders are preachers. That is, the Campbellites rightly deny the distinction the Presbyterians make between ruling and teaching or preaching elders. We will discuss the Scripture claimed further on.

That you may never be deceived on this point, and that you may know how to meet the issue as it is likely to come up often in your ministry, I will let some of the leading lights state Campbellite church government. Prof. McGarvey in answering a question propounded by S. D. Hanna of Temple Texas, in the "Apostlic Guide," Sept. 15, 1885, says:

"Every member of the congregation is in subordination to its eldership as rulers. Members begin preaching under their direction and continue preaching by their permission. Should the eldership decde that they can prove efficient elders or evangelists, they set them apart to their proper work by 'fasting, prayer and laying on of hands.' They grant no other license."

This clearly states that the elders are rulers, and that the congregation is in subordination. They are not agreed, however, as to ordination of preachers, but are agreed in the first statement.

I next introduce a quotation from the "Christian Leader," the date of which is not now at hand, but which will not be called in question:

"Whatever authority Christ left with the church was vested in the elders. There was no higher earthly authority in the churches than that found in he eldership. Shepherds and pastors mean the same thing. Hence, pastors, overseers and elders, being used interchangeably, apply to the same class of officers in the congregation. Beyond this class of officers, there is no ruling power.

" Now let us see the relation that subsists between the overseers and the membership. By choosing these men to rule over them, the congregation pledge themselves to honor and obey these men—according to the word of God. The members, by choosing these men, delegate to them the authority to rule over them, to feed them with the unadulterated word of God, and exercise discipline. After this ruling power has been delegated to the overseers, elders, pastors, the members have no business to interfere with their action. The overseers, governmentally represent the congregation. In a case of discipline, the overseers examine and pronounce upon the case according to the law and testimony, without any dictation from the members, although at the same time it is the privilege of the overseer to consult the wise men of the church in difficult cases, and receive suggestions and advice from them. The election of elders by the congregation precludes all voting on the part of the members. The overseers report to the congregation the action they have taken in a given case, whether it relates to discipline, the employment of a preacher, or the regulation of the Sunday-school, and unless an appeal is taken, the decision stands approved by the congregation without the need of a vote."

From this and much more like it, I conclude that their church government is a Congregational Episcopacy.

I have never been able to get them to affirm the Scripturalness of their church government in debate, or to deny ours.

In a law-suit in Louisville the church government question was involved, and they were compelled to make a statement to the court. It seems there was difficulty in getting the statement, as it would look like a written creed. The editor of the "Courier-Journal" introduced the matter as follows:

"THE ORIGINAL CREED.

"The original, unmodified 'creed' which Mr. Lyons sends for publication with his communication, has already been published by the 'Courier-Journal,' and has been commented upon by the church papers more or less. In order that those who are so deeply interested in the trouble in this church may understand the point at issue between the two correspondents, the original 'creed' is appended. It was modified into what was printed yesterday."

As questions were involved that we are not now discussing, I will quote only the part apropos:

"When a law has been broken by any member of the church, the elders of the church must take cognizance of the fact; they must summon the offender, call for the witnesses and examine the evidence .... For the congregation to vote whether they will sustain or not the decision of the elders, under such circumstances, must strike every thoughtful man as a subversion of all law and order. It is a fatal mingling of two departments of government, and is but a prelude to its destruction.... The decision of the elders, then, is final in all cases of discipline; and good order demands that, instead of voting on the action of their officials, the congregation shall ratify such action by standing while the sentence of withdrawal is read by the President of the Board of Elders in behalf of the church.... In no case shall any subject of discipline be debated or decided in the presence of the congregation.

Think of free (?) men and women, slavishly and ignorantly "standing," to "ratify" a verdict they know not, and the reasons for which they have not been allowed to hear debated. Is that Baptistic? I quote further: Resolution No. 6—"That the right of petition to redress grievances is inalienable, and must not be denied the people, but good order demands that all such petitions be addressed and prepared for the inspection of the elders of the church, and that the practice of irresponsible persons getting up petitions at their pleasure and thus endangering the peace of the congregation can not be too severely reprobated by the church, and that all such persons should be considered as walking disorderly."

Resolution No. 4 allows any "experienced member" to present to the Board of Elders the names of suitable persons for the pastorate, and the above resolution forbids " irresponsible persons" from getting up petitions. Of course the Board of Elders decides who are "experienced members" and who are "irresponsible persons." It strikes me that "irresponsible persons" are idiots, and it may be that the " irresponsible persons" are largely in the majority. I give you this in contrast to the church government of the New Testament that you may appreciate the more that wisdom that came down from above.

The following two clippings from Dr. A. C. Dixon of New York are worth preserving:

" A BOOK SUPPRESSED.

"The Bampton Lectures for 1888, delivered by Edwin Hatch, were suppressed in England by authority. These lectures were entitled 'The Organization of the Early Christian Churches.' The reason why these lectures were suppressed was because they destroyed the foundations on which certain ecclesiastical authority had been reared in modern times. The more thorough becomes our knowledge of the ancient church the more simple becomes its organization, and the less pretense we have for our claim to any temporal authority established by Christ."

" THE CROSS AND DEMOCRACY.

" As the church attains its true work and position, the polity of fraternal democracy must become more and more its working basis. The first democracies in the history of the world were built on the principles of Christianity. There were no democracies before Christ. Greece and Rome were not democracies. They were not even republics. The Grecian world, when Greece ruled the world, was divided into two classes—Greeks and barbarians. The barbarian had no rights. He was a brute, the beast of burden for the oligarchy that called itself Grecian. When Rome was mistress of the world, the world was divided into two classes—Roman citizens and slaves. The slaves were butchered for the Roman populace. It remained for the principles of Christianity to work out in the history of the world the first democracies we have ever known. The history of the cross has been the center around which has clustered the world of human freedom. The cross of Jesus Christ has been the advance herald of liberty, equality, fraternity, wherever the principles of Christianity were taught—class distinctions were undermined at their very foundation. As the kingdom of Christ progresses, all such artificial distinctions must at last be destroyed."

So far from the church being in subordination to elders of any sort, the Scriptures clearly put the elders under subordination to the church. 1 Cor. xii. 28, and v. 12, 13, clearly settles this: "And God set some in the church, first apostles, secondly prophets, thirdly teachers, then miracles, then gifts of healings, helps, governings, various kinds of tongues." "For what have I to do with judging those who are without? Do not ye judge those who are within? But those who are without God judges. Put away that wicked man from among yourselves." The first puts all in and none over the church, and the second shows that the church has judgment of all within. Eph. iv. 11, 12. states that he gave apostles, prophets, evangelists, pastors and teachers, not to rule the church, or to subordinate its members, but to perfect the saints and to edify the body of Christ. This is the opposite direction from subjugation.

In Acts xi. 1-4, we find that Peter had gone a little too far or too fast to suit the lay members of the church and they called him to account. Like a servant as he was, he rehearsed the matter in order from the beginning: "Now the apostles, and the brethren who were in Judæ, heard that the Gentiles also had received the word of God. And when Peter went up to Jerusalem, they that were of the circumcision contended with him saying, Thou wentest in to men uncircumcised, and didst eat with them." After giving them full account of himself the church was satisfied, as we find in verse 18: "When they heard these things, they held their peace, and glorified God, saying, So then, to the Gentiles also God has given repentance unto life."

If Peter had been a pope he might have offered them his big toe to kiss or anathema. If he had been a modern "bishop" he might have reminded them of their duty to "submit their wills to the will of their godly superior." But being a servant of the church and a disciple of Jesus Christ, he reverently bowed to the constituted authority.

In Acts xi. 22 we find the church sending forth Barnabas to do service according to her bidding: "But the report concerning them came to the ears of the church which was in Jerusalem; and they sent forth Barnabas as far as Antioch." When Apollos had been taught the way of the Lord more perfectly by a man and his wife—private members—and desired to pass into Achaia, "the brethren wrote, exhorting the disciples to receive him." (Acts xviii. 25-28). In 1 Cor. xvi. 10, 11, Paul urges the church to let Timothy "be with them without fear" to "conduct him forth in peace." What is this but subordination of the ministry to the church? Read also 3rd John ix. 10 for another example.

Chapter XXIII.

Perhaps there is no better place in this discussion to consider those Scriptures that speak of "rulers" or "ruling elders," and then the one passage on which Presbyterians have built their government out of two classes of ruling elders, one that rules only, and one that rules and teaches. First, those that speak of some one as a ruler. (Rom. xii. 8.) "He that ruleth with diligence." Or he that ruleth let him do it with diligence. The word in dispute translated rule, is proisteemi. It occurs eight times. Six of these are the passages to be examined. It is twice translated maintain. "Be careful to maintain good works" (Titus iii. 8), and "let ours learn to maintain good works." (Titus iii. 14). It is here used in the sense of leading. Emphatic Diaglott has the first "excel in good works," and the other "stand foremost in good works." The margin of the Oxford says for both places "profess honest occupations." So of many others. Certainly the idea of ruling is not in these passages, but of leading. But as the Oxford and King James were predominated by episcopacy, we may expect to find a leaning that way. In the other six passages we will see how those who believe in ruling elders give their testimony. If they explain away the only six passages they have, we may rest assured that this Distinguishing Doctrines of Baptists is not contradicted by these Scriptures.

Returning to the first occurrence of the word in Rom. xii. 8, we note first that the Bible Union has "presides" for "rules." Broadus, Hovey and Weston has, "he that leads." American Commentary in note says: "Most expositors think church overseers are here referred to, though, as Alford says, they seem to be brought in rather low down in the list. Godet thinks that church officers have been already referred to under the term ministry." Joseph Angus says: "He that protecteth" (probably succoreth strangers). Compare ch. xvi. 2. Geo. W. Clark to the same effect. This so far is Baptist testimony, and the Baptist position is stated. Do those holding the other doctrine confirm our interpretation? The Campbellites believe in ruling elders, yet Mr. Campbell in Living Oracles translates "presides." Rotherham has it, "he that takes a lead." Murdock, Presbyterian, in his Syriac Translation has a "presider," with marginal note, "standing at the head." Emphatic Diaglott has "president."

Let this suffice for this passage. We will introduce other testimony further on. The prefix pro does not mean over, but before. The word without the prefix occurs about 170 times and never expresses the idea of ruling. The next passage is 1 Thess. v. 12: "And we beseech you, brethren, to know them which labor among you, and are over you in the Lord." Episcopacy glories in having some one ruling over God's saints. So in Acts xx. 28 they have two overs—overseers over the church. I suppose seeing over was not enough, they must mistranslate so as to get the overseers to rule over as well. It was Episcopalians who represent James in Acts xv. 19 as saying "my sentence is," when he said no such thing. He had no more authority to pass the sentence than any other member of the church. The "sentence" or "decree" (Acts xvi. 4) was passed by the whole church, as any one can see. But to the Scripture, 1 Thess. v. 12, Murdock translates: "We entreat you, my brethren, that ye recognize them who labor among you and who stand before your faces in the Lord." Living Oracles has "preside over you." So has Rotherham. Doddridge says "preside over, or moderate in your assemblies." Moderators are not confined to official elders of any sort, nor do they make their own laws to govern the body. Nor are leaders, if that be the meaning, confined to official elders.

The next passage is 1 Tim. iii. 4, 5, 12. The qualifications of bishops and deacons are given. "One that ruleth well his own house, having his children in subjection with all gravity; for if a man know not how to rule his own house, how shall he take care of the church of God?" Verse 12: "Let the deacons rule their own houses well." Here the word seems to indicate authority. God did give parents authority to execute his law in family government. Children must be under subjection, and to no one so proper as their parents, who, if they have even natural instinct, will rule them in love. So the hen governs her brood and the beasts their offspring. No man has a right to govern his children any other way. "Fathers, provoke not your children to wrath, but bring them up in the nurture and admonition of the Lord" (Eph. vi. 4). The law of the Lord must be the guide in the government of the family. Not so, however, in the church, if episcopacy is the government, for that is against the law of the Lord. But notice the remarkable transition from family to church relations. If a man know not how to rule or preside over his own house, how shall he take care of the church of God?

Whatever authority there may be in the word, and is admissible in family government, must not be so construed in church government. Hence the change from "ruling" the house to "taking care of the church." Why was not the word repeated so as to bring the same kind of authority from the family to the church? The answer is plain. If the word may express authority in the family, it must not express it in the church. The word for taking care is used in two other places—Luke x. 34, 35: "Brought him to an inn and took care of him." "And when he left he told the host to take care of him." That is what a bishop ought to do for a church. He must take care of its spiritual interests and not rule over it. Murdock has "guide the house" in both verses. Rotherham has "presiding well" in both places. So have B. U. E. D. and B. H. and W.

The next passage is the only foundation for Presbyterianism, and to that we will give more attention. "Let the elders that rule well be counted worthy of double honor, especially they who labor in word and doctrine." (1 Tim. v. 17). Here the last three authors quoted have "preside well." Rotherham has "well-presiding elders." Murdock, "elders who conduct themselves well." Living Oracles, "let the seniors who preside well." The Presbyterian, McKnight, has "preside well." This is certainly a toning down of the authority exercised by ruling elders.

Schaff says, pp. 530-1: " These passages forbid our making two distinct classes of presbyters, of which one, corresponding to the seniors or lay elders in the Calvinistic churches, had to do only with the government, and not at all with the administration of doctrine and the sacraments, while the other on the contrary was devoted entirely or at least mainly to the service of the word and altar. Such a distinction of ruling elders, belonging to the laity, and teaching presbyters, or ministers proper, first suggested by Calvin and afterwards further insisted on by many Protestant (especially Presbyterian) divines, rests, indeed, on a very judicious ecclesiastical policy, and is so far altogether justifiable; but it can not at all be proved from the New Testament or church antiquity, and presupposes also an opposition of clergy and laity which did not exist under the same form in the apostolic period. The only passage appealed to in support of this is 1 Tim. v. 17. This 'especially,' we are told, implies that there were presbyters also, who officially had nothing to do with teaching, and that the teaching presbyters were of higher standing. But this conclusion is by no means sure, as may at first sight appear." p. 529.
...."It by no means shows the existence of such presbyters was regular and approved by the apostles, which is the main point. Nay, unless we would involve Paul in self-contradiction, we must suppose the very opposite. The latest commentators on the Pastoral Epistles, Dr. Huther (1850), and Weisen-

ger (1850), also deny that these passages prove the existence of ruling lay elders as distinct from ministers." p. 530. ...."The conclusion from all this is, the presbyters or bishops of the apostolic period were the regular teachers and pastors, preachers and leaders of the congregation.... This by no means authorizes us to suppose that there were two distinct kinds of presbyters and two separate offices of government and doctrine." p. 531.

Barnes, good Presbyterian authority, in his comment on this passage, says: "It cannot, I think, be certainly concluded from this passage that the ruling elders who did not teach or preach were regarded as a separate class or order of permanent officers in the church."

Dr. Cunningham, late principal of New College, Edinburgh, high Scotch Presbyterian authority, says upon this passage: "Some keen advocates for presbytery, as the word is now understood, on the model of John Calvin, have imagined they discovered this distinction in the words of Paul and Timothy. Here, say they, is a two-fold partition of the officers comprised under the same name, into those who rule and those who labor in the word and doctrine; that is, into ruling elders and teaching elders. To this it is replied, on the other side, that the 'especially' is not intended to indicate a different office, but to distinguish from others those who assiduously apply themselves to the most important as well as the most difficult part of their office, public teaching; that the distinction intended is not official, but personal; that it does not relate to a difference in the powers conferred, but solely to a difference in their application. And to this exposition, as by far the most natural, I entirely agree." (Wardlaw on Independence, p. 218).

Dr. Schaff says again on page 496: "The distinction of teaching presbyters or ministers proper and ruling presbyters or lay-elders is a convenient arrangement of the Reform churches, but can hardly claim apostolic sanction, since the one passage on which it rests only speaks of the two functions in the same office."

Matthew Henry says: "They had not, in the primitive church, one to preach to them, and another to rule them, but ruling and teaching were performed by the same persons, only some might labor more in the word and doctrine than others."

So away goes the foundation of Presbyterian church government. And mark well, this fall of their Jericho walls is from the blasts of their own trumpets. I know they also lay a feeble claim on the council in Acts xv., but that will be noticed under another head. The most plausible support for Episcopacy or Presbytery is found in Heb. xiii. 7, 17. Let us look thoroughly into those passages and then we will proceed with three other items included in church government, viz.: The Parity of Ministers;

The Churches the Custodians of the Doctrines; and The Churches the Custodians of the Ordinances. This will close our discussion of Church Government.

CHURCH GOVERNMENT.

CHAPTER XXIV.

Heb. xiii. 7, 17, 24 are now to be noticed: "Remember them which have the rule over you, who have spoken unto you the word of God: whose faith follow, considering the end of their conversation." "Obey them that have the rule over you, and submit yourselves: for they watch for your souls, as they that must give account, that they may do it with joy, and not with grief: for that is unprofitable to you." "Salute all them that have the rule over you, and all the saints."

In these passages a terrible strain is put on three words to sustain the idea of Episcopacy. Our interpretation of them must harmonize with the teaching of Scripture on the subject, and the easiest and most natural translation of the words will harmonize. The word translated "rule over" occurs twenty-eight times in the New Scriptures and is translated "rule over" only in these three places. Mark that fact. It is translated "esteem" in the following places: Phil. ii. 3: "Let each esteem other better than themselves." This was addressed to the bishops and deacons as well as to the saints. In 1 Thess. v. 13

it is too close to the other word translated rule and which has been noticed. If both had been translated rule it would run thus: "Know them which labor among you and are over you in the Lord, and admonish you; and to rule over them very highly in love for their work's sake." This would have been a back action sort of rule, hence instead of "rule over" they translate "esteem." Heb. xi. 26: "Esteeming the reproach of Christ greater riches." The idea of rule over is not in the word esteem. It is translated "count," which is equivalent to esteem in the following places: Phil. iii 7, 8: "Those I counted loss. Yea I count all th.ngs loss, and do count them dung." The idea of rule over is not here. 2 Thess. iii. 15: "Yet count (esteem) him not an enemy." 1 Tim. i. 12: "He counted (esteemed) me faithful." 1 Tim. vi. 1: "Count (esteem) their own masters worthy." Heb. x. 29: "Hath counted (esteemed) the blood of the covenant." Jas. i. 2: "Count (esteem) it all joy." 2 Pet. ii. 13: "They that count (esteem) it pleasure." 2 Pet. iii. 9: "As some men count (esteem) slackness;" verse 15: "Account (esteem) the long-suffering of our Lord." It is translated "think," which is the equivalent of esteem, in Acts xxvi. 2; 2 Cor. ix. 5; Phil. ii. 6, 2, and 2 Pet. i. 13. In Heb. xi. 11 we have: "She judged (esteemed) him faithful who promised." In Phil. ii. 3 we have: "Yet I supposed (esteemed) it necessary." In Luke xxvi. 26 we have: "Let him that is chief be as he that doth serve." I don't object to those that are highly esteemed serving, but I do object to their ruling. In Acts xv. 12 Paul is referred to as the chief speaker, that is, the one most highly esteemed. In Acts xv. 22 Judas and Silas are called chief men among the brethren, i. e., the most highly esteemed, with no reference to their having any ruling power. Phil. ii. 25: "I supposed (esteemed) it necessary." In Acts vii. 10 Pharaoh made Joseph governor over Egypt and all his house. Note, Joseph ruled Pharaoh's house just like he did Egypt, i. e., by the power of esteem. I suppose there never was a governor whose rule was so unlike modern Episcopacy. In the same sense it is said in Matt. ii. 6 that out of Bethlehem should come a Governor that should rule Israel. Christ's rule is on the principle of esteem. "If ye love me keep my commandments." These are all of the twenty-eight places the word occurs. In the light of these, how strange and strained are the translations "rule over" in the three passages in Hebrews first quoted. It could not have been done but by men influenced by Episcopacy, and all revisions that retain it must have been overshadowed by the same influence. I know the noun occurs twenty-two times and is translated governor twenty times and ruler twice, but never is such a ruler or governor in the church. If the word expresses authority outside it must not inside, for Christ said, Mark x. 42-44: "Ye know that they which are accounted to rule over the Gentiles exercise lordship over them; and their great ones exercise authority upon them. But so shall it not be among you: but whosoever will be great among you, shall be your minister. And whosoever of you will be the chiefest, shall be servant of all." Instead of "rule my people Israel" it should be "shepherd my people."

As this criticism has not been raised before, so far as I know, I will add the definitions of a few classical lexicons that we may have the secular use of the word. Grove defines it, "To lead, guide, conduct, direct; to teach, instruct; to preside, rule, govern, reign; to think, deem, esteem." That is all he has. The use of rule, govern, reign, come after the seventh definition. So any of the first seven would be more natural and correct unless the context requires the lower definitions, which we will look into. Donnegan defines, "To go before; to head; to precede; to point out or lead the way; to point out any place to any one; to lead, lead forth, command an army or fleet." This puts command still further down the list of definitions. Pickering defines, "To go before; to take the lead; to conduct, guide; to act as guide; to march before; to point out the road; to command an army." Command a remote meaning again.

Of course a New Testament lexicon, like a dictionary, is influenced by usage. Webster defines baptism rightly, but he must also give the usage of the word whether that usage is right or wrong. So Thayer in giving us a New Testament lexicon must give us the New Testament usage, that is, of the Authorized Version, and he follows this, right or wrong. This he has to do. But here are his definitions: "To lead; to go before; to be a leader; to rule, command; to have authority over." These three passages in the Authorized Version of Heb. xiii. compelled him to give the latter definitions.

In distinguishing this word from its synonyms he says, "it denotes a more deliberate and careful judgment.....a subjective judgment;" (not subjecting judgment). So it is exceedingly strained, taken in the light of its definitions, or of general teaching of Scripture, to translate this word so as to have some one in authority ruling over God's saints. I don't believe it.

But we have another source of light. If those were rulers with subjecting authority, then we must expect the word that expresses a subjective obedience; such as servants render to their masters, children to their parents, disciples to their Lord, and the winds and waves to their ruler. But it is not such a word. The word is Peitho, and if it ever means obedience it is not obedience to authority, but the obedience of trust and love, such as masters may render to their servants, parents to their children, and husbands to their wives. Such obedience is very common, but it is never obedience to authority. The word occurs fifty times and is translated persuade twenty-two times, trust ten times (once in the very next verse, the 18th, "for we trust we have a good conscience)." It is translated "have confidence" nine times, and "obey" six times, and one of those, Gal. iii. 1, is spurious, leaving five out of fifty-five to contend for. The first two are in Acts v. 36, 37. One Theudas and after him one Judas persuaded a number of people to follow them, as false leaders are still doing. And having confidence in them and trusting them, or confiding in them, they are persuaded by them. They did not exercise authority and the obedience was not to authority, but influence. The same word, in the same chapter, and almost the next verse, is translated "agreed." Gamaliel persuaded them to let the apostles alone, and to his proposition they agreed, for he was not commanding them, but persuading them. So obey unrighteousness in Rom. ii. 8 is the influence of enticing lusts. They didn't have to do it, else they would not be responsible. In Gal. v. 7 we have "obey the truth," but the connection and the whole epistle requires trust or confidence in the truth as the true idea. The tenth verse has: "I have confidence in you," using the same Greek word, and no microscope can see obedience to authority in that. The only place out of the fifty-five that obey can be insisted on is in James iii. 3: "We put bits in the horses' mouths that they may obey us." Having taken lessons under four or five famous horse tamers, I have no difficulty in this place. The whole theory of horse taming, and it is the correct one, is not to subject your horse to your authority, but get him to have confidence in you, and to trust you, and you can persuade him to do what you want. This can be seen in the dog and pony show. A great horse lecturer said that a horse will run at the slip of a bridle, not because he is mean, but because he is afraid. Teach him to be governed by words and he will not run when the bridle slips, as he can still confide in you to guide him or lead him.

But another word is involved, "Obey them that have the rule over you and submit yourselves." The word translated "submit" occurs nowhere else in the New Testament. The simple word eiko, however, is used in Jas. i. 6, 23 and translated in both places "is like:" eikoon, the noun, occurs twenty-three times everywhere translated image. Grove defines the verb "to assimilate, liken, make like; to yield, submit, give way." Of course the prefix hupo means render, and submit may be the best rendering, but it must not be submission to authority. Paul said (Gal. ii. 5): "To whom we (eiko) gave place by subjection no not for an hour." He administered a terrible rebuke to the Corinthians for doing this in 2 Cor. xi. 20: "For ye endure it if a man bring you into bondage, if a man devour you, take of you, exalt himself, or even smite you on the face." I would translate, Confide in those leading you and imitate or follow them, for they watch for your souls, etc. Rotherham has it: "Be yielding to those guiding you and complying, for they are watching for your souls," etc. Other translations modify the text more or less. Why Baptists have so long submitted to this rendering I know not, unless there is a general thirst for authority among our preachers. I have known some to use this text in support of ministerial authority. But I suppose they thought it really taught it.

I was giving an exegesis of this text some seventeen years ago to the West Kentucky and Tennessee Ministers' Meeting, and a Presbyterian preacher challenged me for discussion. I need not say I yielded. In the discussion he used this text in support of ruling elders. He traced the ruling eldership back through the Jewish Church and on into heaven, claiming the four and twenty elders before the throne in the succession. I asked him if he claimed the ruling elders of the Jewish Church as Presbyterian elders. He made his argument on the identity of the Jewish and Christian Church, claiming them as Presbyterian elders. I replied that we would so translate a few passages. Mark viii. 31: "And he began to teach them that the Son of man must suffer many things, and be rejected of the Presbyterian elders and of the chief priests and scribes, and be killed, and after three days rise again." Matt. xxvi. 35: "Then assembled together the chief priests and the scribes and the Presbyterian elders, and consulted that they might take Jesus by subtilty and kill him." Mark xiv. 43: "And immediately, while he yet spake, cometh Judas, one of the twelve, and with him a great multitude with swords and staves, from the chief priests and the scribes and the Presbyterian elders." Matt. xxvi. 67: "And they that laid hold on Jesus led him away to Caiaphas, the high priest, where the scribes and the Presbyterian elders were assembled." Matt. xxvii. 3: "And Judas, which had betrayed him, when he saw that he was condemned, repented himself, and brought again the thirty pieces of silver to the chief priests and Presbyterian elders, saying, I have sinned in that I have betrayed innocent blood. And they said, What is that to us? See thou to that." Matt. xxvii.: "But the chief priests and Presbyterian elders persuaded the multitude that they should ask Barabbas and destroy Jesus." Matt. xxvii. 41: "Likewise also the chief priest with the scribes and Presbyterian elders mocked him, saying, He saved others, himself he cannot save." Matt. xxviii. 12: "And when they were assembled, with the Presbyterian elders, and had taken counsel, they gave large money to the soldiers, saying, Say ye, His disciples came by night and stole him away while we slept." Acts xxiii. 14: " And they came to the chief priests and Presbyterian elders, and said, We have bound ourselves under a great curse that we will eat nothing till we have slain Paul." Acts xxiv. 1: "And after five days Ananias, the high priest, descended, with the Presbyterian elders and with a certain orator named Tertullus."

The effect can be better imagined than described

Chapter XXV.

Having turned aside to negative some opposing doctrines, we now take up the affirmative argument. I had it in mind to make a more vigorous protest against Episcopacy than I have done, but as I desire to close this discussion with the year, I am compelled to desist. We have seen that the church itself should elect its own officers, temporary and permanent; should receive, exclude, and restore its own members, and that ministers, like other members, are in the church and subject as other members to church discipline and church authority. I will mention here three exceptions to the general rule favorable to the minister. First, he has all authority as a mouthpiece for God to rebuke sin, privately and publicly: 1 Tim. v. 20: "Them that sin rebuke before all, that others also may fear." 2 Tim. iv. 2: "Preach the word; be urgent in season, out of season; reprove, rebuke, exhort with all longsuffering and teaching." Titus ii. 15: "These things speak, and exhort, and reprove with all authority. Let no one despise thee." Second, an Elder is not to be rebuked: 1 Tim. v. 1: "Rebuke not an Elder, but entreat him as a father." Third, in the matter of accusation he is to be favored. 1 Tim. v. 19: "Against an Elder receive not an accusation, but before two or three witnesses." These are necessary to his protection, as in rebuking sin he is likely to give offense.

THE PARITY OF THE MINISTRY.

is our next proposition. The Catholics and Methodists have several grades in the ministry, from pope to priest, and from bishop to local preacher. This is positive disobedience to divine precept and inspired example. "Ye are all brethren" is Christ's rebuke of that very doctrine.

But let us examine some of the inspired examples which speak plainer than words. If at first there were grades in the ministry, I suppose Paul would rank higher than Barnabas. Barnabas is once called an apostle, but this was in the general and not in the official sense. Apostles, elders, ministers, deacons are all spoken of in both of these senses. If it be said that Christ's rebuke was to a class, and that it simply meant that they were all brethren as apostles, and these were of equal rank, and that it does not prove there were not to be subordinate grades, we will confine our notice to those of supposed different grades. Paul had no authority over Barnabas: Acts xv. 36-41: "And after some days, Paul said to Barnabas, Let us return now, and visit the brethren in every city where we proclaimed the word of the Lord, and see how they do. And Barnabas intended to take with them John also, who was called Mark. But Paul thought it proper not to take with them him who departed from them from Pamphylia, and went not with them to the work. And there arose a sharp contention, so that they parted one from the other, and Barnabas took with him Mark and sailed away to Cyprus. And Paul, having chosen Silas, went forth, being commended by the brethren to the grace of the Lord. And he went through Syria, and Cilicia, confirming the churches." Here Paul makes a proposition to Barnabas: "Let us go again and visit our brethren in every city." A pretty big proposition for those times, and it involved great sacrifice. But note, Paul did not command Barnabas. That he dared not do, as we plainly discover the liberties of Barnabas further on. In verse 37 we see that Barnabas had a will of his own like unto the horn of a unicorn. He determined to take his nephew, John Mark. But Paul did not agree with him, and he gave the ground of his opposition (v. 38). Here was a clash of wills which grew into a quarrel, and the contention became so sharp that it separated them. Paul could not force Barnabas nor Barnabas Paul. They were both free and equal so far as authority is concerned. Each one followed his own purpose, chose his own companion, and each took his own course and went where and when he pleased. There was no general conference and general assembly controlling these preachers. In other words there were no Catholic, Methodist or Presbyterian preachers in those days, nor for hundreds of years afterward.

As Peter is supposed by some to have the preeminence, let us see if he exercised it over Paul, as Paul was "the least of the apostles and not worthy to be called one:" Gal. ii. 11–14: "But when

Cephas came to Antioch, I withstood him to the face, because he stood condemned. For before certain ones came from James, he ate with the Gentiles; but when they came, he drew back and separated himself, fearing those who were of the circumcision. And the rest of the Jews also dissembled with him, so that Barnabas even was carried away with their dissimulation. But when I saw that they walked not uprightly according to the truth of the gospel, I said to Cephas in the presence of all: If thou, being a Jew, livest after the manner of Gentiles and not that of Jews, how dost thou compel the Gentiles to Judaize?" Here the supposed Pope blundered and acted the hypocrite, as the word translated "dissimulation" shows. Peter was older than Paul and was an apostle before him. Paul, amid dangers at Jerusalem, hid, perhaps, in Peter's house for fifteen days. We can imagine a close attachment from this circumstance. But notice the ninth verse. It is not Peter, James and John as usual, but James, Peter and John. So if there was any primacy at Jerusalem at that time, James had it, and not Peter. But when this supposed pope came to Antioch, he left all of his supposed authority behind him. He sinned before all, and caused others to sin. So Paul, his equal in authority, and superior in character, rebuked him before all, and convicted him before all. "They did not walk uprightly according to the truth of the gospel." If Paul had dissembled, it would have been Peter's duty to rebuke him. So the Peter-primacy is seen to be the folly of a fable.

Now put on your magnifying glasses and see if you can discover the so-called ministerial grade in Paul and Apollos: 1 Cor. xvi. 12: "And concerning Apollos the brother, I besought him much to come to you with the brethren; and it was not at all his will to come at this time, but he will come when he shall have opportunity." Let us remember that Paul planted the church at Corinth, and he cared for them as his spiritual children. He tried to keep them supplied with a preacher, which was hard to do for such a quarrelsome church. Some were for Apollos and some for Paul. Those for Apollos greatly desired and preferred him, and if Paul had been afflicted with some of our modern mean and contemptible jealousy, he would have tried to keep him away; and if he had had the authority, he no doubt would have done so. But he was not cut after that little pattern. On the contrary he greatly desired him to go, and it is evident in the superlative degree, that if he had had the authority he would have sent him. When the myriad-minded and lion-hearted Paul greatly desired a thing, it meant something. It meant that the thing would be done if he could do it. But could he do it? He could make kings tremble on the throne, and stop the mouths of lions, but he could not send Apollos to Corinth. Why? Because first, Apollos was a Baptist preacher, and these kind can't be sent; and secondly, Paul was a Baptist preacher, and hence he did not want to send. Apollos had a will as well as Paul, and while it may not have been as strong as Paul's will, yet it was too strong for Paul to force, if he had been disposed to try it. Paul greatly desired him to go at a certain time, but it was not Apollos' will at all to go at that time. They did not differ about the going, for they agreed on that. They only differed as to the time. There was a great difference between them on a very small matter. The "I greatly desired" was not about the going, but the time of the going. Over against that we have a great big "but." Apollos was not half inclined to go at that time, but "it was not his will at all to go at that time." His will was all his own. Paul did not influence that at all, with all of his great desire and powerful persuasion. Apollos not only had a will of his own, but he had business of his own, and that business was all his own, and it was none of Paul's business. Paul, I suppose, was full of his own business, and did not want the responsibility of any other. He left that for presumptuous fools. Ah! here is the answer of a free man. Having been pressed with all the power of powerful Paul he says: "It is not my will at all to go at this time, but when it suits me I will go." Paul had neither power nor authority to move his will "at all," that is, not in the least. The contest was between Paul's desire and Apollos' will, and Apollos' will was too much for Paul's "great desire." If Paul had tried his will instead of his great desire, I have no doubt but that there would have been a repetition of that other "sharp contention" and "separation." I feel like shouting: Hurrah for Paul! Hurrah for Barnabas! Hurrah for Apollos! For it is evident that they called no man Master on the earth. And whoever has a man-Master is a slave, not to be contemned, but to be pitied, and to be rescued and delivered, with all the earnestness there is in us.

Let us test this Ministerial Parity in another case. Paul writes to Titus as his son in the common faith: Titus i. 4. He was Paul's "partner and fellow-helper." But he acted always like a free man, big or little, young or old, "of his own accord." Hence God could work in him to go, and to do the pleasure of his will. Can God do that for the so-called men who trot around at the command of men? Suppose God should "put the same earnest care in the heart" of a Methodist preacher to serve a certain people in a certain place. Could God's "working in" cut any figure in the case? Not as long as he is a Methodist preacher. He prefers a bishop to order him without any inward working.

But to the Scripture showing not the rule of authority, but the rule of recognized fraternity and equality between Paul and his son Titus: 2 Cor. viii. 16, 17: "But thanks be to God, who puts the same diligence for you into the heart of Titus. For he accepted indeed our exhortation; but being very zealous, he went forth to you of his own accord."

Note, God is to be thanked for the service Titus rendered to the Corinthians. God worked in his heart this "earnest care" or diligence. In addition to this as a human instrumentality Paul exhorted him, for he dared not command him. In the third place, Titus being a free man didn't need even Paul's exhortation, "but being more forward or very zealous, he went of HIS OWN ACCORD." Let the words be written in letters of gold and put in a picture of silver. God worked in him the earnest care, and then he went of his own accord. That states a principle that is worth more to this world "than the sun, the center of light; the air, the element of life, the earth, the mother of wealth." Those are physical and temporal, while this is spiritual and eternal.

Chapter XXVI.

Having decided to close this discussion with this chapter, I must treat the last topic briefly. The last two topics previously named I combine into one, viz., THE CHURCHES ARE THE CUSTODIANS OF THE DOCTRINES AND ORDINANCES OF THE GOSPEL. That is to say, the responsibility of "keeping safely all things whatsoever Christ commanded" is made obligatory on all baptized disciples IN CHURCH CAPACITY. The commission in Matthew settles this. If there is any question as to the words "in church capacity," my only answer is that Christ ordained that all baptized disciples should thus act. The Acts of the apostles and the precepts of the Epistles make this plain enough to an honest enquirer. This will be proved as we proceed.

The first great heresy requiring church action is recorded in Acts xv. This should be read with the last three verses of the fourteenth chapter. It is too long to quote here. The church at Antioch, the mother Gentile church, had sent out Paul and Barnabas on a missionary tour, and on their return they assembled the church and made their report of the great things God had wrought with them. It is worthy of note that the church sent them out, and that they reported to the same on their return. What is this but a recognition by the church of her responsibility to have the gospel preached and the ordinances administered in all the world? If there are men in these days too large to be sent out by a congregational church (and there is no other kind), and to report their work back to the church, then they must esteem themselves larger than the Apostles Paul and Barnabas, and in every way too large to be clothed with the gospel armor.

While Paul and Barnabas tarried with the home church for a long time, there came some self-appointed teachers from the church at Jerusalem, saying it was needful to circumcise the Gentile converts and to command them to keep the law of Moses or they could not be saved. It seems, moreover, they claimed to be sent out with that doctrine by the church at Jerusalem. The expression in verse 24, "To whom we gave no commandment," indicates they were not sent by the church at all, for the church in its answer shows her jealous custodian care of the faith, and of course would not have sent the heretics whom she repudiates.

After Paul and Barnabas, the faithful watch dogs "had no small dissension and disputation with them," the church at Antioch decided to send them to the church at Jerusalem where the inspired apostles and first elders had their membership, and thus to settle this question of doctrine. It was necessary that all the churches should hold the same doctrine, and church comity made it easy for churches to consult with each other. The church at Antioch did not ask Paul and Barnabas to decide the question, but to go to the church at Jerusalem and ascertain if they were really holding the doctrine these men were trying to foist on them. And being sent forward by the church (the church of course paying expenses and wages), they preached as they went and "caused great joy unto all the brethren" in Phenice and Samaria. Of course if there had been a pope at Jerusalem or diocecan bishops in these provinces they would not have thought of troubling the common people with their doctrinal disputations. When they arrived at Jerusalem, "they were welcomed by the church, the apostles and elders." While the apostles and elders were expected to do most of the talking, the church was expected to judge and decide the question. So when Peter arose to speak, he did not address the apostles and elders, but he addressed "the brethren," a term used in contradistinction from the officers. (See verse 23, "The apostles, elders and brethren," etc). Then all the multitude became silent and listened to Barnabas and Paul. This shows that the multitude had a right to speak, but through courtesy to the visiting brethren gave them the floor. Also when James, who is thought to have been pastor of the church, arose to speak, he addressed the same class, for he knew also that the settlement of the question was with the church and not with its officers. But let me say again that James in the 19th verse did not say, "Wherefore my sentence is." That is an Episcopalian forgery. "My sentence is" is not in the Greek—not a word of it. The sentence or verdict was not in his power, and he knew it. It was with those whom he addressed—the church—and he only gave his opinion or judgment about what sort of answer should be sent to the Antioch Church. His recommendation, however, was more acceptable to all than Peter's, and hence verse 22 says: "Then it seemed good to the apostles and elders, with the whole church, to send chosen men of their own company," that is chief men among the brethren; not chief men among the apostles or elders, and they sent them, not to a pope or bishop, but to "the brethren of Antioch," etc. In this I claim another proof for Congregationalism. Now these apostles and elders and the whole church write a letter and sign it apostles, elders and brethren, and the "we" and "us" in that letter have these three classes for the antecedent noun, showing that the brethren or whole church had as much interest and authority in settling the doctrinal question as the officers of the church. The little ripple caused in this place by the text of Westcott & Hort, followed by the Oxford Revision, having " apostles and the elders, brethren," with " elder brethren" in the margin, cannot here be discussed. Suffice to say that Broadus, Hovey & Weston follow the A. V. in the text, with "elder brethren" in the margin. The Vatican has Kai before brethren, and the context is too strong to be broken by the conflicting discrepancies on the absence of Kai in Westcott & Hort. The first pronoun in verse 23 will hold it against all caviling—" and they wrote." Who wrote ? " The apostles and elders with the whole church," wrote. The 23rd verse is anchored to the 22nd with an anchor " sure and steadfast." Now watch the six occurrences of " we" and " us" in the letter they wrote, and see if you are not compelled to pass through the first " they" of the 23rd verse to " the apostles and elders with the whole church," of the 22nd verse. Add to this the " brethren" who were addressed by both Peter and James. Acts xv. 22-31: " Then it seemed good to the apostles and the elders, with the whole church, having chosen men from themselves, to send them to Antioch with Paul and Barnabas; namely, Judas called Barsabas, and Silas, leading men among the brethren. And they wrote by them; The apostles and the elders and the brethren, to the brethren from the Gentiles throughout Antioch and Syria and Cilicia, greeting: Forasmuch as we have heard, that some who went out from us troubled you with words, subverting your souls, to whom we gave no charge; it seemed good to us, having become of one mind, to choose men and send them to you, with our beloved Barnabas and Paul, men who have hazarded their lives for the name of our Lord Jesus Christ. We have sent therefore Judas and Silas, who themselves also by word of mouth carry you the same message. For it seemed good to the Holy Spirit, and to us, to lay upon you no further burden except these necessary things; that ye abstain from things offered to idols, and from blood, and from things strangled, and from fornication; from which if ye keep yourselves, it will be well with you. Farewell. They therefore, being dismissed, came down to Antioch; and assembling the multitude they delivered the letter. And having read it, they rejoiced at the exhortation."

We will here take the testimony again of the great Dr. Schaff, the leader of the American Committee of Revisers, Christian Church, p. 510: "They were not to lord it over the flock, but to shine before it as patterns of holy living; to serve it, to control it by its own free convictions; to pay due regard to its rights in all things. This was the course even of the apostles themselves. Almost all the epistles, with their introductions, exhortations and decisions on the weightiest points are addressed, not to the officers alone, but to the whole congregation (589). Nay, even in controversies which concerned all Christians, the apostles did not decide by themselves, but called the congregation (at least frequently) in consultation. We have a striking example of this in the council at Jerusalem, for settling the great question about the binding authority of the Mosaic law and the terms on which the Gentiles were to be admitted to the privileges of the gospel. Here the apostles assembled with the elders and brethren; the deliberations are held in the presence of the whole congregation.... The whole congregation joins in passing the final resolution, and the written decree of the council goes forth, not in the name of the apostles only, but also in the name of the brethren generally, and is addressed to the collective body of the Gentile Christians in Syria and Cilicia."

Dr. Plumptree says on this passage: "The latter words (with the whole church) are important as showing the position occupied by the laity. If they concurred in the letter it must have been submitted to their approval, and the right to approve involves the power to reject and probably to modify."

Bishop Cotterill says: "Not only were the multitude present, but we are expressly told that the whole church concurred in the decision and in the action taken upon it." (Genesis of Church, p. 379).

When Judas and Silas arrived at Antioch, they gathered the multitude together and delivered the letter to them, and when the multitude had read the epistle they rejoiced for the consolation. This shows that the multitude of the disciples at the other end of the line were the ones interested in the settlement of the question.

There are many other Scriptures to the same effect, but only a few can now be quoted without comment. Remember to whom the letters were addressed. They were the responsible parties. Rom. xvi. 17: "Now I exhort you, brethren, to mark those who are causing divisions and occasions of stumbling, contrary to the teaching which ye learned; and turn away from them." Phil. i. 27: "Only let your conduct be worthy of the gospel of Christ; that whether I come and see you, or remain absent, I may hear of your affairs, that ye stand fast in one spirit, with one mind striving together for the faith of the gospel." 2 Thess. ii. 15: "So then, brethren, stand fast, and hold the instructions which ye were taught, whether through word, or through letter of ours." 2 Thess. iii. 6, 14: "Now we charge you, brethren, in the name of our Lord Jesus Christ, to withdraw yourselves from every brother walking disorderly, and not after the instruction which ye received from us." "And if any one obeys not our word through this letter, mark that man, to keep no company with him, that he may be made ashamed." 1 Tim. iii. 15: "But if I delay, that thou mayest know how thou oughtest to conduct thyself in the house of God, which is the church of the living God, the pillar and ground of the truth." Jude 3: "Beloved, while giving all diligence to write to you concerning our common salvation, I found it necessary to write to you exhorting you to contend earnestly for the faith delivered once for all to the saints." Also Rev. ii. 15, 16; 24, 25.

There are many more Scriptures showing that the absent Lord looks to his churches to keep the faith, including the ordinances as they were "once for all delivered;" not to councils, popes or prelates, but "to the saints"—the laity—the whole church, assembled in any place; and a church not thus assembled is a myth. Sometime after he left the earth he conferred again with his constituent authority. What was it? The seven churches which were in Asia. If he were to confer again he would do likewise, unless he erred before and had been converted from the error of his way.

My two lectures on Church Perpetuity, which with the others were requested for publication, are withheld for the present; but I trust soon to give them with good measure. To all who heard or may have read, fare ye well.

ERRATA

Only such as affect the sense will be noticed. The most important caused by misplacing the first two lines on p. 30. They should be the 3rd and 4th lines on p. 29.

P. 16, last line, change "with" to "unto."

P. 20, line 7, "rock" should be omitted.

P. 50, line next to bottom, change "version" to "Scriptures."

P. 51, lines 13 and 14, change "Pal" to "Paul," and "haxe" to "have."

P. 58, line 10, change "him" to "them."

P. 59, last line, change "revised" to "reversed."

P. 68, third line from bottom, omit comma after "feelings."

Chapter 15 should be headed "Church Constitution."

Chapter 18 should be headed "Church Government."

Some dozen lessor errors are committed to the charity of the reader.

A
Biographical Sketch
of
Joseph Burnley Moody
(1838-1931)

BY

JOHN FRANKLIN JONES

A Biographical Sketch of Joseph Burnley Moody (1838-1931)

Joseph Burnley Moody—pastor, author, editor—was born in Clarksville, Virginia June 24, 1838, the son of William A. and Emily Royster Moody. Brought up on a farm, Moody taught and merchandised in young adulthood (*ESB*).

He professed faith in Christ and was baptized into the Bethel Church, Christian County, Kentucky, in July 1855. He was ordained September 11, 1876 by Pewee Valley Church, Oldham County, Kentucky. Educated at Bethel College, Kentucky, he received a D.D. degree in 1891 (*ESB*).

Moody served as the pastor of several churches in Kentucky, Tennessee, Arkansas, Texas, and Florida. The churches included Pewee Valley, Kentucky (1876-80); Lagrange, Kentucky (1877- 80) (*ESB*); Ell Creek, Kentucky (1877-80) (Lasher); Harrod's Creek, Kentucky (1879-80); Paducah, Kentucky (1880-82) (*ESB*); Trezavant, Round Lick, Shop Springs and Martin, Tennessee (1883-86); P. Gilead and S. Central, Memphis, Tennessee (l888) (Lasher); Gilead and Bagdad, Kentucky (1889) (Grimes); Overton, Kentucky (1890-92) (*ESB*); Hot Springs, Arkansas (1893-94); Sunset Church, San Antonio, Texas (1895-96) (Grime); Tampa, Florida (1897-98); and Hot Springs, Arkansas (1899-1902) (*ESB*).

JOHN FRANKLIN JONES

He was editor of *Baptist Gleaner* (1882-86), *The Baptist* (1886-89), and *The Baptist and Reflector* (1889) (*ESB*). Moody wrote prolifically. Among his published works are the following books: *Debate on Baptism, and the Work of the Holy Spirit: in Which the Place of Baptism in the Gospel Economy, Its Design, and the Work of the Holy Spirit in Conversion Are Considered* (1889); *Baptist, Why and Why Not* (1900); *The Distinguishing Doctrines of Baptist* (1901); *The Twelve W's of Baptism* (1906); *My Church, Its Character and Perpetuity* (1908); *My Church* (1908?); *After Death* (1910); *Rights and Restrictions of Women in the Churches; or, Paul Harmonized with the Law and the Gospel* (1910); *The Perfect Gospel* (1922); and *The Exceeding Riches of the Manifold Grace of God* (n.d.) (Starr).

Many of his pamphlets, articles, and sermons are extant. They include: "The Nashville Debate Between Moody and Harding" (1899) (Lasher), "The Name Christian" (1883-85); "Baptist Authors Vindicated," (1889); "Vindication Concerning and Containing the Anderson Letters" (1894); "The Culpability of Ignorance, An Address on 1 Cor. 15:38" (1894); "Baccalaureate Sermon Preached at Ouachita College June 3, 1894" (n.d.); "The Two Covenants" (1896); "The Barren Fig Tree, The Fruitless Christian" (1910); "Church Government," in *The Baptist and Reflector* (1901): 131-206; "Co-operation of Churches: Speeches Nov. 16, 1901, Little Rock, Arkansas" (1902); "The Seven Sabbaths" (1910?); "Address to Gospel Mission Brethren" (1910); "Baptismal Regeneration" (1910); "Baptism and Remission" (1912); "Atheism; Immoral and Irrational" (lectures delivered over eight states, urged for publication) (n.d.); "Sin, Salvation, and Service" (n.d.); "To the Gospel Mission Baptists" (n.d.); "The New-free Woman" (n.d.); "Valid Baptism" (supplemental to "The Twelve W's of Baptism," considered the baptism of anti-missionaries) (n.d.); and "Why Baptist? Why the Church? Why a Baptist?" (n.d.) (Starr).

Moody married Jennie L. Jones December 22, 1895. The marriage was blessed by four children (Grimes). He died in Jacksonville, Florida September 8, 1931 (*ESB*).

BIBLIOGRAPHY

Encyclopedia of Southern Baptists. S.v. "Moody, Joseph Burnley," by Leo. T. Crismon and James Brewer.

Starr, Edward C., ed., *A Baptist Bibliography Being a Register of Printed Material By and About Baptists; Including Works Written Against the Baptists.* 24 vols. Chester, PN: American Baptist Historical Society, 1953. S.v. "Moody, Joseph Burnley, 1838-1931."

Grime, J. H. *History of Middle Tennessee Baptists with Special Reference to Salem, New Salem, Enon and Wiseman Associations.* Cave City, KY: N.p., 1902.

Lasher, George W., ed. *The Ministerial Directory of the Baptist Churches...* Oxford, OH: Ministerial Directory Co., 1899.

BY JOHN FRANKLIN JONES
CORDOVA, TENNESSEE
JULY 2006

THE BAPTIST STANDARD BEARER, INC.

a non-profit, tax-exempt corporation
committed to the Publication & Preservation
of the Baptist Heritage.

CURRENT TITLES AVAILABLE IN
THE BAPTIST *DISTINCTIVES* SERIES

KIFFIN, WILLIAM	A Sober Discourse of Right to Church-Communion. Wherein is proved by Scripture, the Example of the Primitive Times, and the Practice of All that have Professed the Christian Religion: That no Unbaptized person may be Regularly admitted to the Lord's Supper. (London: George Larkin, 1681).
KINGHORN, JOSEPH	Baptism, A Term of Communion. (Norwich: Bacon, Kinnebrook, and Co., 1816)
KINGHORN, JOSEPH	A Defense of "Baptism, A Term of Communion". In Answer To Robert Hall's Reply. (Norwich: Wilkin and Youngman, 1820).
GILL, JOHN	Gospel Baptism. A Collection of Sermons, Tracts, etc., on Scriptural Authority, the Nature of the New Testament Church and the Ordinance of Baptism by John Gill. (Paris, AR: The Baptist Standard Bearer, Inc., 2006).

CARSON, ALEXANDER	Ecclesiastical Polity of the New Testament. (Dublin: William Carson, 1856).
BOOTH, ABRAHAM	A Defense of the Baptists. A Declaration and Vindication of Three Historically Distinctive Baptist Principles. Compiled and Set Forth in the Republication of Three Books. Revised edition. (Paris, AR: The Baptist Standard Bearer, Inc., 2006).
BOOTH, ABRAHAM	Paedobaptism Examined on the Principles, Concessions, and Reasonings of the Most Learned Paedobaptists. With Replies to the Arguments and Objections of Dr. Williams and Mr. Peter Edwards. 3 volumes. (London: Ebenezer Palmer, 1829).
CARROLL, B. H.	*Ecclesia* - The Church. With an Appendix. (Louisville: Baptist Book Concern, 1903).
CHRISTIAN, JOHN T.	Immersion, The Act of Christian Baptism. (Louisville: Baptist Book Concern, 1891).
FROST, J. M.	Pedobaptism: Is It From Heaven Or Of Men? (Philadelphia: American Baptist Publication Society, 1875).
FULLER, RICHARD	Baptism, and the Terms of Communion; An Argument. (Charleston, SC: Southern Baptist Publication Society, 1854).
GRAVES, J. R.	Tri-Lemma: or, Death By Three Horns. The Presbyterian General Assembly Not Able To Decide This Question: "Is Baptism In The Romish Church Valid?" 1st Edition.

	(Nashville: Southwestern Publishing House, 1861).
MELL, P.H.	Baptism In Its Mode and Subjects. (Charleston, SC: Southern Baptist Publications Society, 1853).
JETER, JEREMIAH B.	Baptist Principles Reset. Consisting of Articles on Distinctive Baptist Principles by Various Authors. With an Appendix. (Richmond: The Religious Herald Co., 1902).
PENDLETON, J.M.	Distinctive Principles of Baptists. (Philadelphia: American Baptist Publication Society, 1882).
THOMAS, JESSE B.	The Church and the Kingdom. A New Testament Study. (Louisville: Baptist Book Concern, 1914).
WALLER, JOHN L.	Open Communion Shown to be Unscriptural & Deleterious. With an introductory essay by Dr. D. R. Campbell and an Appendix. (Louisville: Baptist Book Concern, 1859).

For a complete list of current authors/titles, visit our internet site at:
www.standardbearer.org
or write us at:

The Baptist Standard Bearer, Inc.

NUMBER ONE IRON OAKS DRIVE • PARIS, ARKANSAS 72855

TEL # 479-963-3831　　　　　　　　　*FAX # 479-963-8083*
EMAIL: Baptist@centurytel.net　　*http://www.standardbearer.org*

Thou hast given a standard to them that fear thee; that it may be displayed because of the truth. — Psalm 60:4

www.ingramcontent.com/pod-product-compliance
Lightning Source LLC
Chambersburg PA
CBHW022058160426
43198CB00008B/275